Who ~~What~~ Is Truth?

Reframing Our Questions for a Richer Faith

by Jeffrey L. Thayne
& Edwin E. Gantt

with a foreword by James E. Faulconer

Verdand
Press

Printed in the United States of America

ISBN 978-1-7337383-3-0

Verdand Press
www.VerdandPress.com

Contents

Foreword

by James Faulconer

Bible readers are often handicapped by a lack of knowledge of Hebrew and Greek, the languages of the original manuscripts. They unknowingly read things into scripture that aren't really there simply because they have no language to go on but their own, even though that was not the language of those who wrote the scriptures. Furthermore, a person can learn Hebrew and Greek but still overlook or misunderstand things because they don't understand the cultures and histories of the times when various scriptures were written. If they do, they are likely to make a mistake similar to the linguistic one. They are likely to understand the things of scripture in terms of their own culture and history; that is, anachronistically.

That mistake is a particularly easy one to make, even for scriptural scholars, since we have inherited an anachronistic way of thinking about such things as history and truth from the Renaissance, and that anachronism has become as omnipresent and invisible to us as water to fish. With the more recent understanding of such things, we implicitly suppose that the new way of thinking is adequate for understanding everything, including the scriptures and prophetic teachings. We, then, read Genesis or the Gospels or Alma as if they were the kinds of books that we would write. We discover in them our thoughts rather than the thoughts of the prophets. We read Genesis, for example, as a quasi-scientific account of the creation rather than as a ritual text designed to remind us that God made the world and, in the process, to help us understand our covenant relationship with him and each other.

That difficulty can be particularly keen for Latter-day Saints even when we are not aware of it. We have received a prophetic Restoration of ancient things, yet because of our immersion in the waters of post-Renaissance thought, we usually use that (modernist) way of thinking to understand ancient things. Almost completely submerged as we are in the modern way of thinking, it is difficult to do otherwise. The danger is, however, that we may be unable to see much of the power of the Restoration if we unthinkingly see it as what amounts merely to another variation on European thought since 1500. After all, the scriptures were written before 1500, and they are not European. We may profoundly misunderstand what the scriptures teach about such things as truth, covenant, sin, and atonement, and we may see complications and paradoxes where there are none.

In *Who Is Truth?*, Jeffrey L. Thayne and Edwin E. Gantt offer important help for this problem. They don't answer the question of how this or that particular doctrine or scripture would be different if we were able to think about the gospel and our lives in more ancient ways. No mysteries are revealed, at least not in the way the word *mystery* is usually used. Instead, they help us think about the ancient way of understanding things and how it differs from our ordinary understanding. Thayne and Gantt give us an overview of how thinking in a more ancient way changes the way things look and, so, changes our understanding. In turn, that new understanding brightens and freshens the gospel.

The understanding of things that Thayne and Gantt suggest is one that has helped me for much of my life. It has deepened my scripture study. It has helped me understand the weight of sin, the meaning of repentance, and the blessing of atonement better. It has helped me recognize the clash between the overarching structure of the modern world and that of the gospel and to find it easier to live the gospel while enmeshed in the world. It hasn't answered all of my questions, but it has made many disappear, such as how there can be changes in Church teachings and how members of the Church can claim to *know* that the Church is true. It has helped me to have the faith—the trust—in God necessary when my understanding fails without asking me to abandon God-given reason.

Dante tells us that the motto inscribed on the gate of hell is "Abandon all hope, ye who enter here." That could also be the motto over the entrance to the conceptual world that has structured our thinking and experience for the last 500 years. For that conceptual world makes faith, ultimately, nothing but irrational belief and religious practice nothing but superstition and magic. In contrast, the motto Thayne and Gantt could use might be "Raise up your hope, ye who enter here." For the view for which they argue is one that makes faith and religion sensible and hopeful.

Preface

Academic authors tend to write defensively. As academics, we often back up every claim with multiple citations and exhaustively defend our work against every conceivable criticism. For this reason, earlier drafts of this book were originally many times longer and included many more citations, quotations, and rational defenses of our point of view. To adapt those earlier drafts for a general audience, we have eliminated most of this.

If you are unconvinced by the perspectives outlined here, do not immediately dismiss them. Instead, explore the articles and books included in the *Further Readings* section at the end of the book. Every claim we make in this book has been made by dozens of other credible scholars. Their more academic treatment of these same issues may be more persuasive to you.

Introduction

We wrote this book for two audiences: (1) Latter-day Saints who are experiencing a crisis of faith, and (2) Latter-day Saints who are not. President Dieter F. Uchtdorf recently observed, "There are few members of the Church who, at one time or another, have not wrestled with serious or sensitive questions."[1] First, we want to dispel a misconception: some members assume that those who experience a crisis of faith must have committed some sort of sin. As President Uchtdorf explains, "Actually, it is not that simple."[2]

Through the years, many of our friends have experienced doubt about the Church and its teachings. In some instances, there were signs that they were living their life in ways that alienated them from the Spirit of God. In other instances, they chose to take offense at something a Church leader said or did. But in other instances, the seeds for their doubt were *intellectual* in nature. (To be clear, this does not mean that the seeds for those doubts are always the result of good scholarship, merely that they are not always the consequence of immoral behavior.)

For example, we have spoken with friends who questioned their faith when they discovered that the temple rituals have changed (in some respects) over the past 150 years. Others questioned their faith when they found statements made by early Church leaders that seemed to contradict current Church teachings. And yet others questioned their faith when they discovered that a particular teaching they thought was unchangeable doctrine turned out to be nothing of the sort.

This has also happened as prophets or apostles teach principles that contradict popular (or even unpopular) political belief systems. Together, we have witnessed dozens of liberal or libertarian friends call into question the spiritual authority of prophets and apostles because of the Church's teachings on sexuality, marriage, abortion, or other controversial political topics. In such cases, they ask, "How can prophets speak for God and yet get things so wrong?"

We have also witnessed conservative friends do the same. For example, a few of our friends questioned their faith when the Church supported non-discrimination policies in housing and employment in the state of Utah, because such policies would have been condemned (or so they think) by prior Church leaders. In such cases, they ask, "How can prophets speak for God if they teach one thing one decade, and then another a few decades later?"

Others have experienced doubt because blessings they thought had been promised to them never materialized. The formula for prosperity and happiness, they thought, was simple: go to church, pray, read the scriptures, attend the temple, and so forth. After all, the Lord taught, "I, the Lord, am bound when ye do what I say" (D&C 82:10). In such cases, they ask, "Why then am I still single, divorced, suffering from mental illness, or a host of other difficult experiences?"

The list goes on. We have talked with friends who were genuinely troubled that we keep our temple rituals private. The "secrecy" surrounding the temple felt "cultish" to them. "If the temple teaches truth," they asked, "Why do we not broadcast that truth to the world?" Yet others have questioned the purpose of the Atonement. They ask, "Why must God require His Son to suffer, just so that we can live with Him?" Yet others noticed that some of the moral codes we live by seem culturally situated, so they began to question their divine origins.

If you have asked *any* of the above questions, this book is for you. Addressing this endless litany of questions (and more) may be a tall order for a single book. But we do this by addressing what they all have in common. Many of our questions may not have answers because they start with the wrong premises—perhaps like looking for the corner of a round room. Elder Dallin H. Oaks explained, "On many important subjects involving religion, Latter-day Saints think differently than many others."[3] Elder Oaks continued:

> When I say that Latter-day Saints "think differently," I do not suggest that we have a different way of reasoning in the sense of how we think. I am referring to the fact that on many important subjects our assumptions—our starting points or major premises—are different from many of our friends and associates.[4]

Not only do our beliefs hinge on different premises, but the premises of our *questions* matter as well. Many of the questions above are rooted in a single premise: They assume that *truth* is a set of abstract ideas or doctrines that never change.

This may seem like common sense, and if so, that is because most of us accept this view unquestioningly. But this may be one of the "philosophies of men" that can subtly change the way we think about the gospel, and ultimately ensare us in doubt. This view has its roots in ancient Greek philosophy. The Greeks saw things that do not change as more fundamental than those that do, and this led them to focus on abstract ideas as "truth."

In the view we articulate in this book, truth is not a set of abstract ideas, but a living, breathing Person who loves us as His children. This view is inspired by Hebrew thought, which did not separate the search for truth from our journey to God. And once we adopt this view—even provisionally—all of our questions change. *Not all of our questions will be answered, to be sure.* But the way we frame the questions will change so that they no longer tilt us towards doubt. We explain how this is so throughout the rest of this book.

If you are *not* experiencing a crisis of faith, this book is also for you. You may yet stumble upon questions of your own. This book may equip you to challenge their premises and inoculate you against the doubt and confusion that often follows for others. In addition, this book may assist you in your conversations with friends and family who *do* have questions about their faith.

But perhaps more important, this book may help you to reframe the way you think about your relationship with God. Our hope is that all of our readers will center their faith more on the Savior Jesus Christ and the covenants they have made with God, and less on abstract lists of doctrine or beliefs. We echo the words of Nephi, who wrote, "For the fulness of mine intent is that I may persuade men to come unto the God of Abraham, and the God of Isaac, and the God of Jacob, and be saved" (1 Nephi 6:4).

In chapter 1, we will explore the central distinction of this book. This chapter will lay out the premises upon which we often ask our questions (*idea*-truth) and upon which we *could* ask our questions (*person*-truth). Chapter 2 will explore the ancient roots of this distinction and why Latter-day Saints should treat Greek philosophy with caution. The remainder of the book will explore how these premises change how we think about the gospel and how we frame our questions.

CHAPTER 1

What if truth is a person?

For millennia, philosophers have wrestled with the question, "What is truth?" The question itself presumes that truth is a *thing* (a "what"). Most of us see truth as a series of ideas that we can grasp with our minds and store in our memory. From this view, we know truth when we have the *right* set of ideas about the world. The right ideas are those that do not change when we have new experiences. In other words, truth describes the universal, unchanging order of things. This is the *idea* view of truth, or what we call "*idea*-truth." The *idea* view of truth saturates modern thought, and most of us accept it unquestioningly.

Nearly two thousand years ago, Jesus Christ challenged this notion of truth. One day, his followers asked, "How can we know the way?" Christ's reply was simple and profound: "I am the way, the truth, and the life" (John 14:6). Christ did not say, "I know the truth," or "What I teach is the truth." He said, "I *am* the truth." Many will say that this is poetic metaphor. But what happens when we take this literally? This means that truth is not a set of ideas, but a divine *person*. In this book, we explore this *person* view of truth, or what we call "*person*-truth."

Some might say that we are reading a whole worldview into a single verse of scripture, but other passages use similar language. The Apostle John wrote, "In the beginning was the Word, and the Word was with God, and the Word was God" (John 1:1). He continued, "The Word was made flesh, and dwelt among us" (John 1:14). This passage was originally written in Greek. The Greek word that is translated as "word" was *logos*, which is also used to refer to the natural, unchangeable order behind the world. Thus, John taught that the natural order behind the world became flesh and *dwelt* with us.

In the Book of Mormon, Alma taught his son Shiblon, "There is no other way or means whereby man can be saved, only in and through Christ. Behold, he is the life and the light of the world. Behold, *he is the word of truth and righteousness*" (Alma 38:9; emphasis added). In this passage, Christ is again referred to as *being* truth.

The New Testament study manual *Come Follow Me* includes the following comment: "The humble, pure, devoted seekers of righteousness found what they were seeking in Him [Christ]"[5]— again, not merely in His words or teachings, but in the person of Jesus Christ. Similarly, President Ezra Taft Benson taught, "Let us never fear truth, but only its misuse. On the contrary, let us love truth above all else—for *God himself is truth*."[6] We can turn this statement on its head, and the meaning remains the same: "Let us never fear God, but only our misuse of Him. On the contrary, let us love God above all else—for *truth is God himself*."

We are not the first writers to interpret these statements and passages literally. James Faulconer, a philosopher at Brigham Young University (BYU), wrote: "Suppose we take that claim [that Christ is the truth made flesh] quite seriously, not immediately dismissing it as metaphor. Then the path and the truth and the force of life are the same thing in Jesus."[7] Richard N. Williams, a psychologist at BYU, likewise noted: "The truth, the word, the understanding, the message from God comes to us not as a [set of ideas], but as a *person*."[8] Much of this chapter—including contrasting terms like "abstract" vs. "concrete" and "universal" vs. "contextual"—is inspired by similar arguments advanced by BYU professors Brent D. Slife and Jeff S. Reber.[9]

The *person* view of truth has roots in the differences between ancient Greek and Hebrew thought. This is significant, because it implies that the point of view we articulate here will be most sensible to those deeply familiar with sacred texts of Hebrew origin, such as the Old and New Testament (and, we will argue, the Book of Mormon). We will explore this more in chapter 2. For now, let's explore some of the differences between *idea*-truth and *person*-truth.

Idea-truth is abstract, while *person*-truth is concrete

Idea-truth is best expressed as a set of abstract ideas. We cannot see, hear, taste, smell, or touch the underlying order of the universe, so we can only talk about it abstractly. Abstract statements often describe a pattern we observe in the world. For example, "It is always wrong to kill innocent people" is an abstract statement. "The circumference of a circle is always twice the radius times ϖ" is another. These abstract statements make claims about the underlying order of the universe. They can be a moral principle, a mathematical theorem, or a law of nature. We can write them on paper or store them in memory.

In contrast, *person*-truth is *concrete*. You can see truth, hear truth, and even *touch* truth. Shortly after Christ's resurrection,

His apostles gathered together in Jerusalem. Christ appeared to them. Here is Luke's account of what happened:

> But they were terrified and affrighted, and supposed that they had seen a spirit. And he said unto them, Why are ye troubled? and why do thoughts arise in your hearts? Behold my hands and my feet, that it is I myself: handle me, and see; for a spirit hath not flesh and bones, as ye see me have.
>
> And when he had thus spoken, he shewed them his hands and his feet. And while they yet believed not for joy, and wondered, he said unto them, Have ye here any meat? And they gave him a piece of a broiled fish, and of an honeycomb. And he took it, and did eat before them (Luke 24:37-43).

Christ embraced His apostles, spoke with them, touched them, and then ate a meal with them. If Christ really is the "truth made flesh," then truth cannot be reduced to an abstract idea or stored away in memory. Even before His incarnation in the flesh, Christ could still be *present* in a way that an abstract idea cannot. For example, a thousand years before Christ's mortal ministry, the brother of Jared spoke with the Savior face to face (as a spiritual being).

This can be quite terrifying. *Idea*-truth, explained C. S. Lewis, "would never come 'here,' never (to be blunt) make a nuisance of itself."[10] But *person*-truth can (and does) intrude on our lives and make demands of us. *Person*-truth can look you in the eye and ask you why you lied to your mother or deprioritized the things of God. Moroni wrote, "I have seen Jesus, and ... he hath talked with me face to face, and that he told me in plain humility, even as a man telleth another in mine own language, concerning these things" (Ether 12:39). That is not something the Pythagorean Theorem can do.

From an *idea* view of truth, we can discover scientific laws or universal moral maxims and admire their intellectual elegance. But we could never call them friends, except perhaps metaphorically. In contrast, *person*-truth can love you, embrace you, and even weep with you. In other words, we can form a relationship with *person*-truth. Conversely, this implies that we could also be *enemies* of truth, in a literal way.

Idea-truth is universal, while *person*-truth is contextual

Idea-truth is seen as *universal*. From this view, not all facts are "truth"—truth consists only of facts that transcend the particularities of history, culture, and experience. *Idea*-truth cannot just be true for us here and now—it must be true anywhere and everywhere, as well as anytime and every time. Statements that fall short of this standard are merely facts to be explained by truths that *do* transcend context. Further, when we write what we know about the law of gravity on paper, our *expression* of the truth exists in a specific time and place. But the law of gravity itself has no time or place. It is everywhere and yet nowhere at all.

In contrast, *person*-truth (the resurrected Jesus Christ) visited a young man named Saul one morning on the side of a road between Jerusalem and Damascus. In this example, truth was in a particular place at a particular time, saying and doing particular things with a particular person. The implications of this are far-reaching: Truth can exist within our context, and it can also address the particulars of our place and time.

Terryl Givens, a noted Latter-day Saint scholar, wrote, "In the Book of Mormon, prayer frequently—and dramatically—evokes an answer that is impossible to mistake as anything other than an individualized, dialogic response to a highly particularized question."[11] Because of this, God's instructions cannot always be reduced to universal maxims. God can institute different laws for different dispensations, and even within the *same* dispensation. Indeed, the Prophet Joseph Smith taught:

> That which is wrong under one circumstance, may be, and often is, right under another. God said, 'Thou shalt not kill;' at another time He said, 'Thou shalt utterly destroy.' This is the principle on which the government of heaven is conducted—by revelation adapted to the circumstances in which the children of the kingdom are placed. Whatever God requires is right, no matter what it is, although we may not see the reason thereof till long after the events transpire.[12]

C.S. Lewis expressed this idea through a fictional character in his book *Perelandra*: "There can, then, be different laws in different worlds,"[13] and also in different times and eras. Similarly, Latter-day Saints are comfortable with a God who might command them to marry multiple women in one generation and then forbid the practice in the next. In one historical context the God of Israel may command, "Thou shalt not kill" (Exodus 20:13). But in *another* context He may direct His prophet Abraham to sacrifice his son Isaac on Mount Horeb (see Genesis 22:1-2). And in yet another context, he may tell young Nephi to slay a drunken and defenseless Laban (see 1 Nephi 4:7-18).

This is not to say that God's instructions are arbitrary or random—context *is* important, and God *has* reasons. In one case, God told Nephi the reasons: it was vital that Nephi and his family have the records of God's covenant with Israel (see 1 Nephi 4:13-17). However, this reasoning works only *within* Nephi's unique context. This rationale would *not* justify similar actions today, unless we have *also* received direct revelation from God.

These sorts of changes make no sense from the perspective of *idea*-truth, especially when they cannot be reduced to a universal principle. But they make perfect sense if we see truth as a *person* who communicates contextualized instructions to his people and acts in response to changing social, historical , and personal contexts. Our trust lies not in universal, abstract principles that we *apply* to differing contexts, but in a Living Truth who dwells *with* us intimately in the here-and-now.

The rituals and ordinances of the Church are rich with symbolism that finds meaning in our historical context. But they could be different in a parallel universe and still be rich with meaning within the historical context of *that* universe. For example, God could have *not* rescinded animal sacrifice, or He could require us to use wine instead of water for the sacrament (see D&C 27:2). Or He could have chosen a different symbol of cleansing and rebirth than baptism. What matters is that these ordinances are given to us from God through revelation, not that they *cannot* be different than what they are.

Idea-truth is unchangeable, while *person*-truth is a moral agent

From the *idea* view of truth, truth cannot be different than it is. It represents not just what *is* the case, but what *must* be the case. In other words, ultimate truth is not just unchanging, it is unchange*able*. This is what makes truth universal. From this view, if we show that something *could* be different (under different circumstances), then it is not fundamental truth. *Idea*-truth has no agency and no *possibilities*.

In contrast, *person*-truth is a moral agent, just like we are. God chooses to do what He does. Anything that God does, He could also *not* do (or do differently). This is important if we want to form a relationship with Him. It is impossible to form meaningful relationships with things that have no agency. What would it mean to say that God loves us, if cosmic, impersonal forces compelled Him to? God's love is meaningful because He does not *have* to love us but chooses to anyway.

Despite this—or perhaps *because* of this—God is unchangingly reliable. *Person*-truth is reliable not because it *cannot* change, but because of God's commitment to us. "Another way to put this," psychologist Brent Slife wrote, "is that the trustworthiness of God and Christ is unchanging, because these divine beings will always *choose* to be trustworthy, not because They are *made* to be trustworthy out of necessity."[14] God is reliable because He has made covenants with us, not because His instructions cannot change across time and place.

In this way, God's reliability is a matter of His character—that is, who He is and who He chooses to be. God is trustworthy because of who He is, has been, and continues to be. To be God *just is* to be unceasingly reliable and trustworthy. As the Israeli philosopher Yoram Hazony put it, in Hebrew thought, truth—that is, *person*-truth or God—is "that which proves, through time and circumstance, to be what it ought."[15] In other words, we know God is reliable and trustworthy because of the way He conducts Himself with us throughout time.

Idea-truth is passive, while *person*-truth is active.

Idea-truth is passive. For example, the Second Law of Thermodynamics cannot come looking for us—it can only wait for *us* to discover *it*. It cannot communicate with us, speak to us, or reveal itself to us. Idea-truth simply exists as it must, unconcerned about our lives, the world, or, indeed, anything at all. In our relationship with *idea*-truth, *we* are the only active and deciding agents.

In contrast, *person*-truth is active. It is not some idea waiting "out there" for us to come and find it. Instead, *person-truth* interacts with human beings on its (His) own initiative and even interrupts us when we are on other errands. A classic example is the story of Saul of Tarsus when he was on the road to Damascus seeking to arrest Christians:

> And as he journeyed, he came near Damascus: and suddenly there shined round about him a light from heaven: And he fell to the earth, and heard a voice saying unto him, Saul, Saul, why persecutest thou me?
> And he said, Who art thou, Lord?
> And the Lord said, I am Jesus whom thou persecutest: it is hard for thee to kick against the pricks.
> And he trembling and astonished said, Lord, what wilt thou have me to do? (Acts 9:3-6)

Christ's personal visit surprised Saul, as well as the news that he (a relentless and dreaded persecutor of Christians) was to be an apostolic spokesman for Christ. The scriptures are as much about the activity of God as they are about the activity of man. Consider the experience of the prophet Enoch. While we presume that Enoch was living a righteous life, he was not seeking a special commission from God:

> And it came to pass that Enoch journeyed in the land, among the people; and as he journeyed, the Spirit of God descended out of heaven, and abode upon him. And he heard a voice from heaven, saying: Enoch, my son prophesy

unto this people, and say unto them—Repent, for thus saith the Lord. …

And when Enoch had heard these words, he bowed himself to the earth, before the Lord, and spake before the Lord, saying: Why is it that I have found favor in thy sight, and am but a lad, and all the people hate me; for I am slow of speech; wherefore am I thy servant? (Moses 6:26-27, 31)

God's response is simply: "I will do as seemeth me good" (Moses 6:32). God is as much an actor in this story as Enoch. The scriptures are full of such stories, such as those of Moses, Noah, Samuel, Alma, and others. In these stories, God actively teaches, warns, and counsels His children. In contrast, it is hard to imagine Einstein having these sorts of conversations with his special theory of relativity.

Furthermore, Truth does not just reach out to prophets, but also to each of us. He gently invites us to deeper and more intimate relationship with Him. C. S. Lewis described his conversion experience in these terms. As an atheist, he did not want to answer to any Divine Being, especially one he felt had done a lousy job governing the world. However, he wrote:

You must picture me in that room … night after night, feeling, whenever my mind lifted even for a second from my work, the steady, unrelenting approach of Him whom I so earnestly desired not to meet. That which I greatly feared had at last come upon me. … I gave in, and admitted that God was God, and knelt and prayed: perhaps, that night, the most dejected and reluctant convert in all England.[16]

Most of us have felt God's hand gently tug us away from forbidden paths and back into His fold. In the book of Psalms, King

David poetically describes the Lord's activity in our lives: "The Lord is my shepherd; I shall not want. He maketh me to lie down in green pastures: he leadeth me beside the still waters. He restoreth my soul: he leadeth me in the paths of righteousness for his name's sake" (Psalm 23:1 3). Certainly there are things we do to invite God into our lives, but *He* can step over the threshold at the door just as eagerly and actively.

Perhaps this is why uneducated people can have a strong relationship with God. Unlike *idea*-truth, our access to *person*-truth is not dependent on our education. This may be one reason why Latter-day Saints embrace a *lay* ministry. Bishops, fathers, mothers, and assigned ministers do not need a university education to receive guidance from God. Our receptiveness to God does not depend on the detail of our field notes or the replicability of our research methods. God can compensate for the inexperience of a new convert or the imprecise language of an unschooled disciple.

Idea-truth can be discovered, while *person*-truth must be revealed.

Finally, the modern world assumes that *idea*-truth is *comprehensible.* We may have a hard time understanding it—most people, for example, struggle to understand quantum mechanics. But from this view, we as a collection of humans will *eventually* figure out the fundamental truths of the universe—with enough study, observation, and thinking. Our methods may not be precise enough *yet.* But from this view, there are no truths that we cannot discover, if we have enough time, resources, and intelligence.

The same is not true of *person*-truth. The scriptures raise the question: "Canst thou by searching ... find out the Almighty unto perfection?" (Job 11:7). In other words, can we know God perfectly through our own efforts? The answer is no. Elder Bruce R. McConkie taught during a BYU devotional, "God is and can be known only by revelation; he stands revealed or he remains forever unknown."[17] The First Presidency also stated, "Man, by searching, cannot find out God. ... The Lord must reveal Himself or remain unrevealed."[18] Similarly, the Book of Mormon prophet Jacob declared: "Behold, great and marvelous are the works of the Lord. How unsearchable are the depths of the mysteries of him; and it is impossible that man should find out all his ways. And no man knoweth of his ways save it be revealed unto him; wherefore, brethren, despise not the revelations of God" (Jacob 4:8).

Consider the ramifications of Jacob's statement: this implies that reason, observation, or any other human strategy can never get at God unless God decides to reveal Himself to us. We learn about God on *His* terms and at *His* discretion. To draw again from the wisdom of C. S. Lewis: "When you come to know God, the initiative lies on His side. If He does not show Himself, nothing you can do will enable you to find him."[19]

This means is that the truth of God is always a *revealed* truth. For example, when the Savior asked Peter, "But whom say ye that I am?" Peter fervently responded: "Thou art the Christ, the Son of the living God" (Matt. 16:15-16). No doubt, Peter reflected over the years of his association with this man of Galilee. But Peter's knowledge was grounded in revelation from God Himself. As Christ said, "Blessed art thou, Simon Bar-jona, for flesh and blood hath not revealed it unto thee, but my Father which is in heaven" (Matt. 16:17).

Not only is *person*-truth grounded in revelation, it sometimes violates the expectations of reason. As God taught Isaiah: "[M]y thoughts are not your thoughts, neither are your ways my ways.... For as the heavens are higher than the earth, so are my ways higher than your ways, and my thoughts than your thoughts" (Isa. 55:8-9). The ideas we form of God through our own reason and observation are always insufficient. "My idea of God," C. S. Lewis explained, "is not a divine idea. It has to be shattered time after time. He shatters it Himself. He is the great iconoclast. Could we not say that this shattering is one of the marks of His presence?"[20] To know God, we must seek direct revelation, and we must be willing to relinquish our expectations.

CHAPTER 2

The ancient roots of *person*-truth

The differences between *idea*-truth and *person*-truth can be mapped onto differences between ancient Greek and Hebrew thought. For many Greek philosophers, truth was abstract and impersonal, while in Hebrew thought, truth was more contextual and personal. These differences still matter today. Modern thought is influenced by the ideals of Greek philosophy. The brilliant mathematician and philosopher Alfred North Whitehead once wrote, "The safest general characterization of the [Western] philosophical tradition is that it consists of a series of footnotes to Plato."[21]

In contrast, the earliest Christian converts (during the apostolic ministry of Peter, James, and John) were more familiar with Hebrew thought. Old Testament scholar Norman H. Snaith wrote, "The Old Testament is the foundation for the New. The message of the New Testament is in the Hebrew tradition as against the Greek tradition. Our tutors [for understanding] Christ are Moses and the prophets, and not Plato and the Academies."[22] Another influential biblical scholar, John Dillenberger, has cautioned, "[T]o ignore Hebraic ways of thinking is to subvert Christian understanding."[23]

Greek Philosophy

The gods of Ancient Greece were very different than the God we find in scripture. The gods of Olympus were more like super-heroes, larger-than-life embodiments of common human virtues and vices. Outside the occasional dalliance or bit of meddling, they were not interested in human affairs and seldom responded to people who worshipped them.[24] When the philosophers of Athens heard Paul's missionary message of a God who was compassionate and involved in human affairs, they responded by calling Paul a "babbler." They said, "He seemeth to be a setter forth of strange gods: because he preached unto them Jesus, and the resurrection" (Acts 17:18).

For Greek philosophers, the quest for truth was more or less unrelated to the legends that were taught in the temples of the cities or at the hearthside in the home. It was not a quest to understand the intentions of divine persons. Rather, it was a quest to capture (via the intellect) certain rational principles or concepts. When Greek philosophers *did* believe in the traditional gods, they believed they operated within a broader universe that was governed by ideas. From the perspective of some, even the gods were bound by fate and could not alter the dictates of impersonal, abstract law.[25] In this way, *truth* was distinct from any god who could carry on a dialogue with mortals.[26]

The ancient Greeks were fascinated with things that do not change. Greek philosophers often disagreed with each other, but they almost always saw things that do not change as more fundamental than things that *do* change. James Faulconer wrote, "[The Greeks] believed that change is a defect, that whatever is ultimate must be static and immobile. What changes, including the world that we experience, is of a lesser order than what does not change."[27] For this reason, they also saw things that are abstract as more important than things that are particular to a specific context, and things that are outside space and time as more valuable than things that are physical and temporal. Greek philosophers analyzed and categorized objects (specific people, places, or things) in terms of unchanging characteristics, rather their specific contexts or features.

Plato (427–347 BC), for example, distinguished between the *substance* and the *essence* of things. The *substance* of a table can change. A table can be brown or black, plastic or wood, varnished or scratched, all while still being a table. However, the *essence* of a table cannot change (without becoming something else instead). For example, something is not a table if it is not somewhat flat and raised off the ground, or if we cannot place objects on it. These attributes are essential to the idea of a table. For Plato, this world of *essences* is where we find *truth*.

Pythagoras of Samos (ca. 570–ca. 495 BC) believed that *truth* could be found in mathematics and that the physical world conformed to universal mathematical laws.[28] From his perspective, before we can understand the world, we must discover the mathematical realities that govern it. Mathematics has the kind of consistency we would expect if fundamental truth is unchangeable. The *Pythagorean Theorem* ($a^2 + b^2 = c^2$) holds true for every right triangle in every context and is just as true today as it was in the days of Pythagoras.*

Aristotle (384–322 BC) focused his attention on the material world in addition to the world of ideas. He argued that we must ground all of our theorizing in the stubborn facts of physical

---

* Well, not exactly. The Pythagorean Theorem only holds true for Euclidean geometry (that is, the geometry of planes). It breaks down entirely in non-Euclidean geometries (such as on a globe). This illustrates the main idea of this book: how the world looks and what counts as truth depends on our starting point.

reality and sensory experience. Aristotle believed that universal laws govern the world and that they will manifest in the predictable operations of the physical universe. To discover truth, from his view, we must carefully observe the world and detect these patterns. Aristotle pointed Western philosophy towards empirical observation (as opposed to philosophical speculation) as the foundation of modern science.[29]

As different as their ideas were, each of these philosophers emphasized the importance of *non-change*. With few exceptions, the ancient Greeks believed that anything that changes is subservient to a higher order that does not change.[30] For that reason, ultimate truth in the Greek worldview is whatever is fundamentally *unchangeable*—whether we are talking about the natural world or human morality.[31] For the ancient Greeks, the genuine truth-seeker sifts through the dynamic variety of life and looks for whatever is the same in every place, every time, and every context.

Hebrew Thought

In this book, we use the term Hebrew *thought* rather than Hebrew *philosophy*. This is because the ancient Hebrews did not engage in the same sort of formal scholarly dialogue as the Ancient Greeks. Rather, the ancient Hebrews explored the same questions through the concrete matters of everyday living. Further, unlike the Greeks, the Hebrews did not place as much emphasis on non-change.

This can be seen in differences between the Hebrew and the Greek languages: Greek tends to focus on what is static and unchanging (the nouns), while Hebrew tends to focus on what is in motion (the verbs).[32] This difference has filtered into modern-day English. Biblical scholar Marvin Wilson provides us with an example:

> The English language usually places the noun or subject first in the clause, then the verb or action-word; for example, 'The king judged.' In the narrative of biblical Hebrew, however, the order is normally the reverse. That is, the verb most often comes first in the clause, then the noun; thus, 'He judged, (namely) the king.'[33]

In Hebrew thought, nouns are not static objects, but are associated with action of some kind. What something *does* defines what it *is*. If we were to think like a Hebrew in the modern day, we might define a car not in terms of its exterior shape, but in terms of its function in our lives: a car is something that transports people from one place to another. If it no longer does that, it is no longer a car. A rusted car found half buried in the woods is an *artifact* (something that reveals the past), but it has stopped being a car.

In English, we often use verbs that convey abstract ideas, such as *love, hate,* or *anger,* that cannot be directly observed. In contrast, the Hebrew language uses concrete imagery and action words to convey abstract ideas. Marvin Wilson provides a number of examples. In Hebrew writing, "[to] 'look' is 'lift up the eyes' (Gen. 22:4); 'be angry' is 'burn in one's nostrils' (Exod. 4:14); 'disclose something to another' or 'reveal' is 'unstop someone's ears' (Ruth 4:4) ... 'stubborn' is 'stiff-necked' (2 Chr. 30:8; cf. Acts 7:51)."[34] Similarly, as Hebrew scholar George Adam Smith explains, "Hebrew may be called primarily a language of the senses. [Words] originally expressed concrete or material things. ... Only secondarily and in metaphor could they be used to denote abstract or metaphysical ideas."[35]

Because the Hebrew language focuses so heavily on the concrete and tangible, Faulconer noted, "Unlike Greek, Hebrew does not conceive of anything immaterial or unembodied, even in thought."[36] Indeed, Faulconer suggests, the idea of the immaterial may even be "required to believe that ultimate reality is absolutely static."[37] For this reason, the Hebrews seldom (if ever) focused on abstract or universal ideas the way that ancient Greek thinkers often did.[38] Wilson explains, "For [the Hebrews], truth was not so much an idea to be contemplated as an experience to be lived, a deed to be done. ... Thus their language has few abstract forms."[39]

In stark contrast with Greek philosophy, there is virtually no search for truth that is distinct from the search for God in Hebrew literature. To the extent that Hebrew thinkers *did* hold abstract ideas, they rarely elevated them to the realm of "truth" in a way that rivaled or transcended God. The Hebrews focused on their covenant relationship with God, and any intellectual journey that did not end with the living God of Israel was a journey in the wrong direction. Indeed, as Wilson pointedly observes, "the dynamic, active presence of the living God is one of the most central unifying themes of the Hebrew Bible."[40]

For the Hebrews, a God who does not judge and intervene in the world is a God who does not meaningfully exist. Even the name Yahweh (Jehovah), which can be interpreted to mean, "I will be there (for you)," implies both activity and relationship.[41] God's *identity* and *being* is defined by His activity towards us. Interestingly, the Hebrew word for truth is *emeth*, which means "faithfulness, firmness, reliability." In Deuteronomy, we read, *"He is the Rock, his work is perfect: for all his ways are judgment: a God of truth and without iniquity, just and right is he"* (Deut. 32:4). The God of Israel is a God of truth because He is without iniquity or betrayal.

In short, the Hebrew perspective does not elevate abstract or impersonal ideas to the realm of the Divine because abstract ideas, by their very nature, cannot *act* in the world—they do not *do*, *change*, or *influence* in the world in any way. For the Hebrews, the God of Israel actively engages with the world, and the world is constantly influenced (and changed) by God's activity. Thus, in a Hebrew worldview, abstract ideas are always one step removed from His relationship with us in the world.

Because ancient Greek philosophers focused on the abstract, they strove for rational and intellectual perfection, logical certainty, and the systematic representation of impersonal truth. In contrast, the Hebrew thinker strove for a concrete relationship with God and specific moral guidance in specific moral contexts. Most important, the Hebrews did not determine right conduct by looking for abstract, universal moral laws, but by consulting the commitments they had made to God and what He had commanded of them. Hebrew morality was shaped by the specific instructions that God gave to Abraham, Isaac, Jacob, Moses, and others.

Clearly the idea of *covenant* was central to Hebrew thinking and practice. However, the Hebrews thought of these covenants not as concepts but as specific commitments made with God by a particular people at a particular place and time.[42] This is why *history* was deeply important to the Hebrews. The Hebrews valued a strict remembrance of God's covenants with man, often through physical, actionable rituals (such as animal sacrifice or ritual cleansing) and communal practices (such as annual feasts and celebrations). These rituals and celebrations preserved in their collective remembrance the promises of God and their commitments to Him.

Another way to illustrate the difference between Greek and Hebrew thought is by comparing Aesop's fables with the parables of Jesus. Aesop (620-564 BC) was an Ancient Greek storyteller who told tales that involved talking plants or animals (such as the Tortoise and the Hare, or the North Wind and the Sun). Aesop's fables were meant to teach moral lessons (usually to children) through stories. The "moral of the story" is usually expressed as a universal maxim or moral principle and is far more important than the story itself. The story is merely a way to illustrate the idea in a memorable way.

In contrast, the parables of Jesus express more than universal maxims or abstract principles. In fact, Jesus's Hebrew audience may not have universalized the lessons of a parable at all. The meaning depends on the life circumstances of the hearer. For example, consider the parable of the prodigal son: sometimes we are the son, other times we are the father, and other times we are the elder brother. In the parable of the lost sheep, sometimes we are the ninety and nine, and other times we are the lost sheep. At yet other times, we are the shepherd.

Parables introduce narratives that we can *live* and *re*live in different ways in the unfolding situations of our lives. All of sacred scripture is the same: passages that mean one thing to a rebellious teenager may have a different meaning for a new parent, and still yet a different meaning for a bereaved spouse. The message cannot be universalized or summarized as a list of principles to follow. The *particulars* of the story matter and are meant to be carried with the hearer (or reader) into his or her varying contexts.

For example, Nephi "likened" the scriptures to his situation by comparing his family's experience to the story of Moses, the children of Israel, and their collective struggle to escape the bondage of Pharaoh. He did not sit down and reason out some sort of universal, abstract principle based on Moses's experience. Rather, he saw himself and his family as the Israelites, Jerusalem as Egypt, Laban as pharaoh, and their journey as from captivity, through the wilderness, toward a land of promise. He brought the story, with all of its rich detail and nuance, into his context.

There is danger in "summarizing" Hebrew thought, precisely because its less-abstract nature tends to resist tidy summation. Nonetheless, it is safe to contrast Greek philosophy's focus on the *abstract* and *universal* with Hebrew thought's focus on the *particular* and the *concrete*. The Greeks valued things that do not change; Hebrew thought emphasizes that which is dynamic and active. In addition, the Greeks separated the idea of truth from the idea of a personal, acting God, while Hebrew thought does not. In Hebrew thought, abstract ideas are less important than our relationship with the God of Abraham, Isaac, and Jacob.

Apostasy and Restoration

A few hundred years after Christ's death, the "fullness" of the gospel of Jesus Christ was no longer taught or practiced in its original, pristine form. Latter-day Saints often refer to this as the Great Apostasy. This apostasy was (at least in part) due to those within the Church who relied on philosophy and reason in lieu of ongoing revelation. Elder Dallin H. Oaks taught that, following the death of Christ, "there came a synthesis of Greek philosophy and Christian doctrine in which the orthodox Christians of that day lost the fullness of truth about the nature of God and the Godhead."[43]

Many scholars refer to this process as the "Hellenization" of Christianity. Because Greek language and culture were profoundly different from Hebrew language and culture, this changed the way scriptural truth was understood. As Thorleif Boman explains:

> Christianity arose on Jewish soil. ... As the New Testament writings show, [Jesus and His apostles] were firmly

rooted in the Old Testament and lived in its world of images. Shortly after the death of the Founder, however, the new religious community's centre of gravity shifted into the Greek-speaking Hellenistic world. ... Not only are these two languages essentially different, but so too are the kinds of images and thinking involved in them. This distinction goes very deeply into the psychic life; the Jews themselves defined their spiritual predisposition as anti-Hellenic.[44]

This development was accelerated by thinkers who wished to reconcile Christian teaching with the commonly accepted Greek ideas of their contemporaries.[45] As early Christians adopted Greek assumptions, they reshaped their understanding of God in far-reaching ways. Because Greek thought prioritizes the abstract and unchangeable, Christian scholars began to think of God as *immutable*, an abstract being without body, parts, or passions who exists outside space and time, everywhere and yet nowhere at all.[46] Elder Oaks taught:

In the process of what we call the Apostasy, the tangible, personal God described in the Old and New Testaments was replaced by the abstract, incomprehensible deity defined by compromise with the speculative principles of Greek philosophy. ... In the language of that philosophy, God the Father ceased to be a Father in any but an allegorical sense.[47]

The result was that the dynamic, living, passionate, caring, and embodied God described in the pages of Old and New Testament (and the Book of Mormon) was replaced by the sort of abstract, unembodied, and timeless entity described in the pages of Plato, Aristotle, and other Greek philosophers.

In this way, the God who could weep with his loved ones at

the tomb of Lazarus (John 11:35), the God who "groaned within himself" and was "troubled because of the wickedness of the house of Israel" (3 Ne. 17:14), and the God whose joy could be full as he called little children to him and blessed them "one by one," weeping yet again (3 Ne. 17:21), became a thing of the primitive past. By the time of the Reformation, the Western world had moved so far away from the living God of the Bible that Martin Luther argued that, even though "God is represented [in the Bible] as being angry, in a fury, hating, grieving, pitying, repenting," nothing of the sort "ever takes place in him."[48]

In short, Latter-day Saints have good reason to be suspicious of Greek philosophy. For example, James Faulconer argues that "Greek … models of thought cannot do justice to the true and living God."[49] In fact, he argues that because of the prevalence of Greek thought in the Western world, "[M]ost of what passes for talk about God, *whether positive or negative*, is talk about a god who is not the God of Israel,"[50] nor the God who appeared to Joseph Smith in the spring of 1820.

As Latter-day Saints, we believe that Christ's Church has been restored in our day through modern revelation. We believe that God the Father and His Son Jesus Christ visited Joseph Smith and anointed him to be a prophet and a spokesman, just as they had anointed Moses, Samuel, and Saul of Tarsus before him. And, in that moment (and on other occasions), Joseph Smith observed the physicality and living *concreteness* of God as the Father and the Son counseled with him face to face and gave him instructions in a particular place and at a particular time—as well as *for* a particular place and particular time.

Through Joseph Smith, God re-established the original apostolic Christian church, complete with divinely appointed prophets and apostles who have been commissioned to officiate covenants with God through sacred ordinances. Joseph Smith was also instrumental in restoring our understanding of God as the concrete, embodied, and relational being worshipped by the ancient Israelites.[51]

For example, the Book of Mormon prophet Nephi declared: "[T]he fulness of mine intent is that I may persuade men to come unto the God of Abraham, and the God of Isaac, and the God of Jacob, and be saved" (1 Nephi 6:4). Likewise, Moroni testified of "a God of miracles, even the God of Abraham, and the God of Isaac, and the God of Jacob; and it is that same God who created the heavens and the earth, and all things that in them are" (Mormon 9:11). The scriptures of the Restoration (the Book of Mormon, the Doctrine and Covenants, and the Pearl of Great Price) thoroughly depict God as the *person*-truth we described in the previous chapter.

CHAPTER 3

Faith in ideas, or faithfulness to a Person?

So why does this all matter? Because the difference between *idea*-truth and *person*-truth changes how we think about faith. When we see truth as a set of ideas, then religion becomes a set of doctrines. For example, when we learn about a religion, we often start by asking, "What do they believe?" However, from the point of view of *person*-truth, faith is much more than a belief in ideas. It is a way of living in *faithfulness* to God (the Truth). From this view, when we learn about a religion, we might ask instead, "How do they live?" Religion becomes a *way of life*, rather than a set of beliefs or dogmas.

When we adopt the *person* view of truth, we have faith in God in the same way we are faithful to our spouses: by making and keeping sacred promises. The focus of our faith becomes our covenants, which includes loving and serving God and our fellow man. We might also covenant to believe certain things (for example, that Jesus is our Lord and Savior). *Believing* is also an action, after all. But the focus of our faith changes from a set of doctrines to our relationship with the Truth made flesh (Christ). Our relationship with this Divine Person changes our priorities and invites us into a life of discipleship.

The vast majority of scripture is not a list of doctrines but a chronicle of God's saving, rescuing, and uplifting activities in the world. This is what we would expect if truth is a person with whom we form a relationship. We justify our trust and faithfulness by sharing stories about our experiences with that person. The scriptures show from past examples that God *has* been faithful and will *continue* to be faithful to us, as well as how we can be faithful to Him.

Again, this has roots in ancient thought. Hebrew thought does not place nearly as much emphasis on abstract doctrine as Greek thought. For this reason, it seems sensible to suggest that a Hebrew worldview values *orthopraxy* (right conduct) over *orthodoxy* (right belief). As William Barrett helpfully explains: "The Hebrew is concerned with practice, the Greek with knowledge. Right conduct is the ultimate concern of the Hebrew, right thinking that of the Greek."[52] This does not mean the Israelites did not sometimes expel heretics or care about doctrine at all—rather, Hebrew thinking simply prioritized action over belief.

What this means is that, from a *person* view of truth, having the right beliefs is much less important than living the right sort of way. A bishop living in Brigham City, Utah, might have some eccentric (and wrong) beliefs about the Atonement but still faithfully keeps his covenants, serves God in his calling, and lives out his faith in an exemplary way. From the *person* view of truth, he is more faithful to Truth than someone who has all the *right* ideas about the Atonement but does none of those things. It is far less important, from this view, that every Church member (and leader) holds the exact same beliefs as everyone else.

Church teachings can change over time

Robert Millet, a professor of ancient scripture at BYU, recounts a story in which a friend of his once exclaimed: "Bob, many of my fellow Christians have noted how hard it is to figure out what Mormons believe. They say it's like trying to nail Jell-O to the wall!"[53] This is because doctrines that were emphasized in some decades have been deemphasized in others. The enormous corpus of sermons and literature written by Latter-day Saint leaders contains (apparent) internal contradictions. To the extent that this is true, it is because doctrine—in the sense of an unchanging, abstract belief system—is not the object of our religious observance. Rather, the object of our faith is the living (and dynamic) God of Abraham, Isaac, and Jacob.

But further, there have now been a hundred (or more) members of the Quorum of the Twelve since the Church was founded, with various backgrounds and perspectives. They have each given dozens of sermons a year in a variety of contexts over their decades of Church service. It would be surprising *not* to find internal contradictions in such a large volume of words from so many people. And from a *person* view of truth, this is not a problem—the purpose of their sermonizing is to invite us into a covenant relationship with God, not to generate a perfect consensus of abstract belief.

Furthermore, the God of the Restoration is, above all else, a God who *speaks*. We do not only have records of what God has *spoken*, we believe that He continually guides His servants today. Nearly everything that we know about Him has the potential to change as He continues to reveal Himself to us. James Faulconer wrote, "Since Latter-day Saints insist on continuing revelation, they cannot have a dogmatic theology that is any more than provisional and heuristic, for a theology claiming to be more than that could always be trumped by new revelation."[54]

In fact, this happened on multiple occasions. In the days following the crucifixion and resurrection of Christ, Peter had a vision in which God commanded him to take the gospel to the Gentiles. This new revelation countermanded a lengthy history in which God's covenant was seen as an exclusive arrangement with the children of Israel. Peter explained to Cornelius, a Gentile convert seeking baptism, "Ye know how that it is an unlawful thing for a man that is a Jew to keep company, or come unto one of another nation; but God hath shewed me that I should not call any man common or unclean" (Acts 10:28).

The prophet Jacob taught in the Book of Mormon that men should only have one wife (except in cases where God commands). The Prophet Joseph Smith taught that God commanded him and others to take multiple wives. President Wilford Woodruff ended the practice of polygamy, and we no longer even *teach* the practice as doctrine today. If we believe that truth is a set of abstract doctrines, this might bewilder us. But if we believe that truth is a *person* who communicates with us within our unique sociohistorical contexts, this becomes more sensible.

When President Spencer W. Kimball announced that blacks would be ordained to the priesthood, contrary to decades of previous Church policy, a few members of the Church lost their trust in Church leadership. They felt betrayed because they believed that Church teachings were *unchangeable*. Elder Bruce R. McConkie was well-known for his controversial attempts to doctrinally justify the old policy. After the change, he said, "Forget everything that I have said, or what President Brigham Young or President George Q. Cannon or whomsoever has said in days past that is contrary to the present revelation."[55]

Idea-truth requires that the shared beliefs of a religion remain consistent across time and context. From this view, teachings that change over time cannot represent *truth*. If God communicates different teachings in different dispensations or cultures, we assume that our communication with God has been disrupted by "interfering signals." If the current prophet contradicts an earlier prophet (or seems to), the authority of *both* prophets is called into question. We assume that the precepts of men have been, either in the past or in the present, passed off as revelation.

However, from a *person* view of truth, it matters much less that living prophets teach the same things as Joseph Smith or Brigham Young (or even prophets half a century ago). We have no need to disparage or dismiss the teachings of past prophets as wrong or foolhardy simply because we no longer practice or teach the same things today. In fact, there is no guarantee that we will find a universal set of doctrines that makes all prophetic teachings perfectly consistent. According to biblical scholar Marvin Wilson,

> To the [Hebrew], the deed was always more impor-tant than the creed. He was not stymied by language that appeared contradictory from a human point of view. Nei-ther did he feel compelled to reconcile what seemed irrec-oncilable. He believed that God ultimately was greater than any human attempt at systematizing truth.[56]

God guides His children *within* their contexts. What was pru-dent for one generation may no longer be prudent for another. His instructions are not the sort of universal, unchangeable abstractions that we privilege in the modern world.

We worship the Living Truth over the dead law

We have witnessed friends question their loyalty to the Church when prophets or apostles have drawn into question their political worldviews. For example, some conservative and libertarian members of the Church questioned the Church's decision to support nondiscrimination policies in housing and employment in the state of Utah. These members used statements by past Church leaders (such as President Ezra Taft Benson and others) to show that current Church leaders must be in error. The *person* view of truth can help us resolve these tensions.

When the Israelites were traveling through the wilderness, they began to criticize Moses and complain about their situation. In response, "the Lord sent fiery serpents among the people, and they bit the people; and much people of Israel died" (Number 21:6). God then instructed Moses, "Make thee a fiery serpent, and set it upon a pole: and it shall come to pass, that every one that is bitten, when he looketh upon it, shall live" (Numbers 21:8-9). Those who looked to the serpent lived, but many chose not to look. Nephi, in the Book of Mormon, tells us that "because of the simpleness of the way, or the easiness of it, there were many who perished. And they did harden their hearts, ... and they did revile against Moses, and also against God" (1 Nephi 17:41-42).

Why would so many Israelites ignore such a simple instruction? They may have thought Moses was violating commandments that he *himself* had delivered from God: "Thou shalt not make unto thee any graven image. ... Thou shalt not bow down thyself to them, nor serve them" (Exodus 20:4-5). Perhaps they thought Moses was a fallen prophet, or that he was testing them to see if they would value their own lives over God's commandments. Either way, the Israelites may have rigidly adhered to what they thought were the unchangeable commandments of God.

In this story, the ancient Israelites may have elevated the *law* over the Law*giver*. That is, they may have prioritized what God had *said* over what God was now *saying*. Perhaps Moses was teaching the Israelites the *person* view of truth, and the need for constant, ongoing communication with God. Perhaps God was teaching the Israelites never to idolize abstract systems of belief over continuing direction from the Living God of Israel.

There is a danger in this, however. Some Latter-day Saints have used these very ideas to rationalize a wholesale rejection of prophetic teaching and warning. For example, some argue that we should not become dogmatically attached to the Proclamation on the Family because the Church will someday adopt a more enlightened view of family and sexuality. Some argue that same-sex couples will someday be able to marry in the temple, just as blacks now hold the priesthood. They rightly point out that prophets are fallible and can make mistakes; they wrongly assert that this means we should reject their current teachings.

As Latter-day Saint blogger J. Max Wilson has pointed out, "Just like fundamentalists who reject the living prophets by following dead prophets, [some] progressives reject the living prophets by following anticipated future prophets."[57] These two groups make the same mistake. They assume that if living prophets contradict dead prophets, then either the living prophets or the dead prophets must have been wrong. But this is only the case if we adopt the *idea* view of truth, which assumes that truth is a set of universal, unchanging ideas. If we adopt a *person* view of truth, then *even if* prophets someday make changes to the Proclamation on the Family, prophets *today* can still be teaching what is right for our times.

We need to clearly understanding what God instructs us to

do, especially if we adopt the *person* view of truth. We do not have to mentally assent to the various rational theologies that members of the Church have sometimes constructed. But we *may* be required to believe that God has asked us to live the law of chastity, or to compassionately feed and clothe the hungry and naked, or to share the gospel with our friends and neighbors. Otherwise, we may believe in a god who asks for different sacrifices and makes different demands of us than the God of Abraham, Isaac, and Jacob. Loyalty to the Truth made Flesh means that we steadfastly teach others what He, through His servants, has taught us.

When we evaluate the teachings of God's servants against our ideological worldview (whether it be liberalism, libertarianism, conservatism, or any other perspective), we adopt the *idea* version of truth. In other words, the problem is not libertarianism, liberalism, conservativism, or any other belief system. The problem was with -*isms* entirely, when those –*isms* lead us to prioritize abstract ideas over ongoing revelation. This can lead to what we call "ideolatry," which is what happens when we elevate an abstract system of belief (or ideology) to the level of "absolute truth."

This is *especially* the case when we become dogmatic about our particular theological perspective, or hold to those perspectives with a fervor that defies correction by God or His servants. When we do this, we have supplanted the living God with an idea (or set of ideas). The God of Israel is not an abstract, universal, immutable set of ideas or laws, but a living, dynamic Person who communicates instructions tailored to our specific time and situation. Latter-day Saints can be flexible in matters of abstract belief while being resolute in matters of loyalty to God.

This does not mean that there are no consistent patterns in God's instructions. We can be confident that some changes— such as repudiating the essentiality of Christ, the reality of divine authority, or the centrality of marriage—would not preserve any sense of continuity in God's revelations across time, and we can safely assume that they will not happen. But a need for some measure of continuity is not the same thing as the absolute *sameness* emphasized by Greek thought or *idea*-truth. The extension of the gospel to the gentiles, and the extension of the priesthood to blacks, can be rendered perfectly sensible in the broader story of God's global church and the ongoing Restoration. Other changes might be more difficult to accommodate in that broader story, or might change the genre of the story entirely.

Reframing Our Questions: Chapter 3

For each of the remaining chapters of the book, we will include examples of how our questions might change if we adopt *person*-truth as the premise of our questions.

Idea-truth: What universal, unchangeable set of doctrines do Latter-day Saints believe?

Person-truth: What covenants have Latter-day Saints made with God, and how does this affect the way they live their lives?

The first question puts the focus on abstract ideas, while the second question puts the focus on living out our covenants with God. Living our covenants with God may involve professing shared beliefs (such as the truthfulness of the Book of Mormon, the divine calling of prophets, the Atonement of Christ), but the emphasis is less on the ideas themselves than it is the way of life they entail (e.g., studying the Book of Mormon, heeding the words of prophets, repenting of sin and relying on Christ).

Idea-truth: How can the Church be true if Church leaders teach something different today than what they taught before?

Person-truth: How can we sustain God's servants as they make inspired adjustments to the Church and its emphasis?

The first question assumes that the litmus test for divine teaching is *unchangeability*, while the second question assumes it is *divine authority and origin*. Those who adopt *person*-truth embrace change when it comes through divinely authorized sources, without necessarily denigrating what has come before. By itself, change does not mean Church teaching is not divinely inspired today, nor that it was not divinely inspired before.

CHAPTER 4

Knowing God vs. believing ideas about Him

When we view truth as a divine person instead of a set of abstract ideas, this also changes how we think about *testimony*. Our personal testimonies become centered on the Savior Jesus Christ, since He *is* the truth. From the *person* view of truth we "know" truth in the same way we might know a beloved friend. It is one thing to know *about* some*thing*, and quite another to *know* some*one*. A man knows his wife in a very different way than he knows the dates of the French Revolution.

In Spanish, for example, the words *saber* and *conocer* are both translated in English as the verb "to know" but mean different things. We would use *saber* when we know something is the case. We would use *conocer* when we know a *person*. A story from an old Latter-day Saint Young Women's manual may illustrate the difference:

> A man died and was resurrected and waiting in a room to be interviewed. Another man was ahead of him. The door opened, the man entered, and the door closed. The man on

the outside could hear the conversation on the other side of the door. The interviewer began: "I want you to tell me what you know about Jesus Christ."

"Well, He was born of Mary in Bethlehem; he lived thirty-three years, spending the last three organizing his church, choosing his Apostles, and giving the gospel to direct our lives."

The interviewer stopped him and said: "Yes, yes, that's all true, but I want you to tell me what you know about Jesus Christ."

"Well, he suffered and died so that we could have eternal life. Three days later he was resurrected so that we might return to Heavenly Father."

"Yes, yes, that is true, but I want you to tell me what you know about Jesus Christ." The man, a little perplexed, again began: "Well, he restored the gospel in its fullness to the earth through Joseph Smith, reorganized his church, gave us temples so we could do work to save our dead. He gave us personal ordinances for our salvation and exaltation."

The interviewer again stopped him and said, "All of what you have said to me is true." The man was then invited to leave the room. After he left the door opened and the second man entered. As he approached the interviewer he fell upon his knees and cried, "My Lord, my God."[58]

The first man in the story treated truth as a set of ideas (or doctrines). The second man, however, had spent his life developing a personal relationship with the Truth. He could do far more than testify that he knows that Christ is real—he could claim to *know Christ*. From this perspective, when we bear witness of God, we do far more than list doctrines that we claim to know are true.

We share experiences we have had with God. We bear witness of His hand in our lives, of His goodness to us, of His saving grace and transforming love.

We often talk about the Holy Ghost confirming to us that the doctrines of the Church are true. When we adopt a *person* view of truth, the Holy Ghost becomes more than a tutor who points us towards abstract truth. He represents and points us towards the divine personage of God. He serves as our Divine companion in lieu of God's actual physical presence with us. Instead of saying, "The Holy Ghost has confirmed these doctrines to me," we might say, "Through the Holy Ghost, *I have come to know God.*"

The distinction is important. When we seek a testimony, our goal is not to add to a list of doctrines that the Holy Ghost has told us are true. Rather, our goal is to develop a relationship with Divine persons. Sometimes, we treat prayer like a Magic 8-Ball, where we ask abstract questions looking for "yes," "no," or "maybe" answers. From this view, we feel doubt when our specific questions do not find answers. But from a *person* view of truth, our hope is to encounter God's hand in our lives and to witness His grace working in our hearts and minds. Our prayers become less focused on confirming abstract doctrines and more on inviting God into the details of our families and communities.

Faith and knowledge are not opposites

The *idea* view of truth separates faith from knowledge. Typically, knowledge is thought of as *justified* belief in truth (abstract ideas), while faith is seen as belief *without* justifying evidence. From this view, beliefs are only *justified* (that is, knowledge) when they are based on repeated, systematic observations of the natural or the social world. For example, famous philosopher and neuroscientist Sam Harris wrote, "Faith is simply *unjustified* belief in matters of ultimate concern. ... However far you feel you have fled the parish, ... you are likely to be the product of a culture that has elevated belief, in the absence of evidence, to the highest place in the hierarchy of human virtues."[59]

The *idea* view of truth sometimes filters into how we make sense of our own faith. In fact, some Latter-day Saints argue that faith cannot exist without doubt. They reject the *certainty* with which many Latter-day Saints express their testimonies of the restored gospel. One Latter-day Saint online commenter (who goes by Brit) expressed this idea well: "Rather than doubt and faith being incompatible, I think that doubt is the *required* environment for faith to exist, for when there is no doubt (uncertainty), there is certainty (knowledge) and hence faith is no longer necessary."[60] Some Latter-day Saint thinkers have begun to use similar logic to valorize doubt and skepticism as a prerequisite to genuine faith. For example, one Latter-day Saint thinker has written: "Doubt isn't a sign of weakness, but of courage. ... It takes faith and courage to take steps when one cannot fully see the path ahead, and faith, in the true sense of the word (i.e., trust), can only be forged alongside doubt."[61]

In contrast, the *person* view of truth shifts our understanding of doubt. If we use marriage as our example, spouses are always and ever *knowing* each other better every day. But it would make little sense to say that each must *question* or *doubt* the existence or faithfulness of the other in order to have faith in him or her or to be truly faithful. A man's fidelity to his wife, after all, is not justified by empirical evidence but by his love for her and the commitments he has made with her. Furthermore, his trust in *her* fidelity does not require that he *doubt* her. Similarly, our fidelity to God is not justified by rational inference or empirical evidence either.

As C. S. Lewis taught:

> To believe that God—at least this God—exists is to believe that you as a person now stand in the presence of God as a person. What would, a moment before, have been variations in opinion, now become variations in your personal attitude to a Person. You are no longer faced with an argument which demands your assent, but with a Person who demands your confidence.[62]

From the *person* view of truth, the opposite of faith is not *knowledge* but rather being *unfaithful*. It is *disloyalty*, or breaking the promises we have made to God, giving ourselves over to other gods and other priorities. When Nephi invited his brothers to exercise faith, he said: "Yea, and how is it that ye have forgotten that the Lord is able to do all things according to his will, for the children of men, if it so be that they exercise faith in him? *Wherefore, let us be faithful to him*" (1 Ne. 7:12). The invitation Nephi extends is not to mere *belief* but to *fidelity*. We think it is the *idea* view of truth that traps us into defining faith as the opposite of certainty, something that *requires* doubt in order to be faith.

We justify our faithfulness through experience with God

James Faulconer noted, "In Hebrew, truth is understood to be 'firmness, faithfulness, trust.'"[63] According to Marvin Wilson, the ancient Hebrews knew "that God was always met in history, in the context of events, in the world of activity and doing. The person of faith was one who was so committed to God that, like Abraham, he ventured into the unknown with the full expectation that God would meet him there."[64] From this view, faith is not unjustified belief in a set of ideas, but a forward motion with full confidence that God will keep his promises. This helps us understand what Moroni meant when he said, "I would show unto the world that faith is things which are hoped for and not seen; wherefore, dispute not because ye see not, for ye receive no witness until after the trial of your faith" (Ether 12:6).

When we place our confidence in God, it is not a blind, unjustified confidence. Rather, it is a confidence born of *experience*. Prophets in scripture invite us to faithfulness by appealing to our memory. For example, Alma warned: "Have you sufficiently retained in remembrance the captivity of your fathers? Yea, and have you sufficiently retained in remembrance [God's] mercy and long-suffering towards them?" (Alma 5:6). Similarly, Captain Moroni asked: "Yea, have ye forgotten the captivity of our fathers? Have ye forgotten the many times we have been delivered out of the hands of our enemies?" (Alma 60:20). Nephi also posed the following questions to his brothers:

> How is it that ye have not hearkened unto the word of the Lord? How is it that ye have forgotten that ye have seen an angel of the Lord? Yea, and how is it that ye have forgotten what great things the Lord hath done for us, in delivering us out of the hands of Laban, and also that we should obtain the record? (1 Nephi 7:9-11)

This is why history was so important to the ancient Israelites—it was how they justified their confidence in God. Similarly, it is within *our* history of modern-day deliverances, miracles, and manifestations that we ground *our* loyalties to God. In addition, we have our own personal encounters with God that date from the moment we first started praying and experiencing God's hand in our lives. We have the witnesses of our family, friends, neighbors, and prophets who have also felt the hand of God in their lives, who tell us that God deserves our confidence. Pressing forward with confidence in God is not an act of mere blind trust, nor is it without any viable evidence.

It is in this light that we strive to be faithful to God—not because we know *about* Him (as in, we possess empirical or rational knowledge of His characteristics or existence) but rather because we *know* Him (as in, we have actual relational experience with Him, both personally and collectively), even if we do not yet know Him perfectly. Belief is certainly important, but the term *faith* connotes much more than simply belief. It is a lifestyle of fidelity to God—we heed His voice and trust in His promises as we patiently live out our own.

Reframing Our Questions: Chapter 4

Idea-truth: "Heavenly Father, is the idea _____ a true doctrine or principle of the gospel?"

Person-truth: "Heavenly Father, is this thy Church and are its leaders thy chosen and anointed servants?"

The first question focuses on whether a particular idea or teaching corresponds to or reflects some abstract doctrinal principle, presumably of the sort that constitute the basis of the gospel of Christ. In contrast, the second question focuses on coming to recognize the hand of God, and His active involvement in selecting, directing, and speaking through His chosen servants, rather than on the abstract truth or falsehood of certain ideas. Rather than seeking to know the truth of abstract ideas, the questioner is seeking to recognize the voice of God in our lives and in Church.

Idea-truth: How can I really know for certain that the doctrinal principles and teachings of the Church are true?

Person-truth: How can I come to know God through the ordinances and community of the Church?

Our modern emphasis on *idea*-truth can often lead us to dwell endlessly on the intractable philosophical problems of epistemology (e.g., how exactly it is we can know what is true of the world?). Focusing on how we can come to know God as a person can radically shift our perspective and the nature of our relationship with God and others.

Idea-truth: What threshold of evidence do I need before I can justifiably say that I know God exists?

Person-truth: Given God's faithfulness to us (as recorded in sacred writ), how can *we* be faithful to *Him*?

The first question also shows concern with achieving epistemological certainty (i.e., absolutely undoubtable knowledge) grounded in an abstract proposition (i.e., God exists). The answer to this question requires the use of logic, reason, or empirical forms of study to establish the objective certainty of the proposition that God exists. If such rational certainty cannot be achieved, then belief in the truth of the proposition "God exists" is reduced to a matter of mere faith (i.e., a hope not justified by reason in any real way). *Person*-truth, on the other hand, invites us to see faith not as belief in a set of ideas, but rather as a way of life, living one's fidelity to God and our promises to Him even in the midst of trials and confusion. Faith in this view is a matter of trust—a trust born of personal experience with God and a willingness to make and keep promises.

CHAPTER 5

Person-truth does not give us control

Why is truth reliable? Why is truth valuable? *Idea*-truth is seen as reliable because it never changes. In contrast, *person*-truth is reliable because He is *good*. *Idea*-truth is seen as valuable because knowing the laws of how the world works gives us control over that world, and our knowledge of *idea*-truth is independent of our moral activities. However, our relationship with *person*-truth is contingent on our moral conduct and may actually require us to relinquish control in our lives.

If truth is found in unchangeable ideas, and if the operations of the physical world are patterned after these ideas, then truth allows us to predict what will happen in future or counterfactual situations. Once we know what could happen if conditions were different, we can exert control over the future by changing those conditions. This is called the "technological ideal" of modern science. Seen in this light, *idea*-truth is valuable because of the *power* that it provides us over our lives.

Further, knowing *idea*-truth is entirely independent of the moral quality of our lives. Our behavior in the bedroom (or the boardroom), our dishonesty and pride, or our lack of compassion towards those who suffer, are all unrelated to our ability to accurately report observations or make logical inferences. For example, is the general theory of relativity undermined because Einstein was unfaithful to each of his wives? *Idea*-truth is entirely a matter of the mind, not of the heart or soul. *Idea*-truth does not care what we plan to do with our knowledge.

Person-truth involves personal morality

In contrast, how we behave towards God and others *does* affect our ability to know *person*-truth. In fact, it is only through obedience to the Truth made Flesh that we come to really *know* Him. Violating God's laws damages our relationship with Him and alienates us from Truth. Joseph Smith taught this quite clearly when he said: "God has created man with a mind capable of instruction, and a faculty which may be enlarged in proportion to the heed and diligence given to the light communicated from heaven to the intellect."[65]

From this view, our ability to understand God's will for us may be jeopardized if we are cruel to others, or if we self-serving. Obviously, an active God can interrupt a life of sin and call us unto repentance, as He did Saul on the road to Damascus or Alma the Younger as he was gadding about trying to destroy the Church. Nonetheless, our capacity to know God depends on our receptiveness to His voice and our willingness to covenant with Him.

Of course, *person*-truth *does* grant us power, but of a different kind than the technological ideal of modern thought. The Book of Mormon prophet Jacob taught that through faith "we truly can command in the name of Jesus and the very trees obey us, or the mountains, or the waves of the sea" (Jacob 4:6). However, it is always and ever *God's* power by which we do this. In the very next verse, Jacob clarifies, "Nevertheless, the Lord God showeth us our weakness that we may know that it is by *his* grace, and *his* great condescensions unto the children of men, that we have power to do these things" (Jacob 4:7, emphasis added).

Clearly, the power of God is not found in our ability to extrapolate future events through unchangeable laws. It is a power grounded in moral goodness and the spiritual possibilities of righteous living. Unlike *idea*-truth, *person*-truth cares what we plan to do with His power. As we read in the Doctrine and Covenants:

> Behold, there are many called, but few are chosen. And why are they not chosen? Because their hearts are set so much upon the things of this world, and aspire to the honors of men, that they do not learn this one lesson—That the rights of the priesthood are inseparably connected with the powers of heaven, and that the powers of heaven cannot be controlled nor handled only upon the principles of righteousness (D&C 121:34-36).

In other words, while *idea*-truth promises to help us exert our will on the world (for good or bad), *person*-truth does nothing of the sort. It is only when we strive to enact God's will (in humility) that *person*-truth shares His power with us.

Person-truth does not help us predict the future

From the *idea* view of truth, we find safety in formulating reliable expectations of the future. In contrast, from the *person* view of truth, our safety is grounded in the goodness of God and

His promises to us. An anecdote from a popular story by C. S. Lewis may help illustrate this point. In his science fiction book, *Perelandra*, Lewis tells a story of an Eden-like ocean world with both floating islands and fixed lands. One of the protagonists, a woman, was commanded by a Divine Entity to spend her nights on islands that float with the currents.

At one point in the story, her companion drifted away on a neighboring floating island, and she did not know when she would see him again. A demonic being tempted her to spend a night on fixed land, promising her that if she did so, she would be better situated to find her lost companion. Lewis's story differs from the Biblical account of Eden, because the protagonist never succumbs to temptation. She is later introduced to fixed land by divine beings, who rescind the prior commandment and reunite her with her companion. At this point, she remarks:

> The reason for not yet living on the Fixed Land is now so plain. How could I wish to live there except because it was Fixed? And why should I desire the Fixed except to make sure—to be able on one day to command where I should be the next and what should happen to me? It was to reject the wave—to draw my hands out of [God's], to say to Him, "Not thus, but thus"—to put in our own power what times should roll toward us. ... That would have been cold love and feeble trust. And out of it how could we ever have climbed back into love and trust again?[66]

Sometimes we apply the technological ideal of *idea*-truth to the gospel. We assume that if truth is a set of abstract ideas that never change, then when we know truth, it will help us form expectations of the future. In this view, gospel living becomes a formula that we follow to guarantee a prosperous life, a happy marriage, faithful children, or any number of other blessings. However, turning to Christ involves surrendering control over our lives. We no longer put "trust in the arm of flesh" (2 Ne. 4:34) or put our hopes and faith in our expectations for the future. Although entirely fictional, the above passage from Lewis echoes the sentiments of the New Testament apostle James, who wrote:

> Go to now, ye that say, To day or to morrow we will go into such a city, and continue there a year, and buy and sell, and get gain: Whereas ye know not what shall be on the morrow. For what is your life? It is even a vapour, that appeareth for a little time, and then vanisheth away. For that ye ought to say, If the Lord will, we shall live, and do this, or that. (James 4:13-15)

Life springs surprises on even the most faithful Saints—an unexpected death in the family, a distressing inability to marry, the terrors of war, the careless mistakes of others, and so forth. We cannot control the future, and *person*-truth promises no such mastery. This does *not* mean we should live life passively or ignore the future when conducting our affairs. It simply means that our faith and trust should rest with God, not our preparations. We use the abstract ideas and patterns of science and technology to advance our own aims and desires, whereas *person*-truth is an end unto Himself.

Person-truth is not safe

Another fictional anecdote from C. S. Lewis's book *The Silver Chair* will help illustrate our point even more. In Lewis's story, the character Jill has for the first time stepped into a magical world in Aslan's own country. Aslan is the Great Lion, the son of the Emperor beyond the sea. All creatures in Narnia are morally accountable to him, and they look to him for guidance. Jill knows nothing of Narnia or Aslan, and she is alone and terrified and extremely thirsty.

In time she stumbles upon a stream, but between her and the stream is a fearsome lion. After waiting some time, hoping for the lion to move away, Jill is stunned to hear the lion speak: "If you are thirsty, you may drink." Jill, with reverential awe, asks, "Will you promise not to—do anything to me, if I do come?" Aslan responds, "I make no promise." The conversation then continues:

> "Do you eat girls?" she said.
>
> "I have swallowed up girls and boys, women and men, kings and emperors, cities and realms," said the Lion. It didn't say this as if were boasting, nor as if it were sorry, nor as if it were angry. It just said it.
>
> "I daren't come and drink," said Jill.
>
> "Then you will die of thirst," said the Lion.
>
> "Oh dear!" said Jill, coming another step nearer. "I suppose I must go and look for another stream then."
>
> "There is no other stream," said the Lion.[67]

While Aslan invited Jill forward to drink from the stream, he offered her *no promise of safety*. Nonetheless, Jill decides to trust Aslan and drink from the stream. Aslan then asks her to go on a quest, and the adventure of the book begins. Lewis offers us a similar insight in another Narnia book, *The Lion, the Witch, and the Wardrobe*. In this story, the Pevensie children find themselves in Narnia in the care of some talking beavers who speak reverentially about Aslan. Upon hearing that Aslan is a lion, the children ask, "Is he safe?" One of the beavers respond, "Safe? [D]on't you hear what Mrs. Beaver tells you? Who said anything about safe?

'Course he isn't safe. But he's good. He's the King, I tell you."[68]

What does it mean that God is not "safe"? We certainly do not mean that God is *dangerous to us*, in the sense that we are imperiled by Him. Rather, it means that God is always capable of surprising us. We cannot ever wrap our minds around God so completely as to be able to anticipate His will for us in all contexts of our lives. Our *ideas* of God are always at risk of being rendered obsolete by God's actual presence and activity in our lives. C. S. Lewis, while writing on his experiences after his wife passed away (who, in the passage below, is referred to as "H"), shares insights that illustrate the difference between a real *person* and our *ideas* about said person. He wrote:

> Today I had to meet a man I haven't seen for ten years. And all that time I had thought I was remembering him well—how he looked and spoke and the sort of things he said. The first five minutes of the real man shattered the image completely. Not that he had changed. On the contrary. I kept on thinking, 'Yes, of course, of course. I'd forgotten that he thought that—or disliked this, or knew so-and-so—or jerked his head back that way.' I had known all these things once and I recognized them the moment I met them again. But they had all faded out of my mental picture of him, and when they were all replaced by his actual presence the total effect was quite astonishingly different from the image I had carried about with me for those ten years. How can I hope that this will not happen to my memory of H? That it is not happening already? Slowly, quietly, like snow-flakes—like the small flakes that come when it is going to snow all night—little flakes of me, my impressions, my selections, are settling down on the image

of her. The real shape will be quite hidden in the end. Ten minutes—ten seconds—of the real H. would correct all this. And yet, even if those ten seconds were allowed me, one second later the little flakes would begin to fall again. The rough, sharp, cleansing tang of her otherness is gone.[69]

In other words, in the absence of the real person, our ideas about a person tend to ossify, settling into familiar patterns until we almost come to believe they are the same thing as the person themselves. However, the mark of being in the presence of a real human being is that our ideas about the person are always at risk of being made obsolete by the *real* person before us. So it is with the distinction between *idea*-truth and *person*-truth.

It is in this way that God is not safe. He is not an abstract idol that we can mold in our own image, or render in our minds along wholly rational, expected, and familiar grooves; rather, He is a real person who can come and dash our mental idols of Him at any time He pleases. As we quoted earlier in the book, C. S. Lewis further wrote, "My idea of God is not a divine idea. It has to be shattered time after time. He shatters it Himself. He is the great iconoclast. Could we not say that this shattering is one of the marks of His presence?"[70]

In the character of Aslan, and in his description of his own experiences with grief, Lewis has beautifully expressed the profound difference between *idea*-truth and *person*-truth. *Idea*-truth is reliable because it is *safe*. Once you genuinely know it, you know what to expect—there will be no surprises. It never changes the rules on you, asks you to sacrifice something dear to you, or holds you morally accountable. *Idea*-truth dispels the mystery of life and nature, allows us to predict what comes next, and brings the world under human control. It is our attempt to enwrap the world of our experience within the folds of reason, so that everything makes sense to us.

Like Aslan, the God of Abraham, Isaac, and Jacob is reliable because He is *good*. However, He is certainly not *safe*. He is not predictable or controllable—or without surprises up His sleeve. Becoming disciples of Christ provides no guarantee against suffering, heartache, grief, or pain (which is precisely what we ask of idea-truth and its companion, the technological ideal of science). As a real person—with that "cleansing tang of otherness" that Lewis describes—He is always and ever able to challenge our conceptions of Him through His ongoing activities in the world. To the extent that person-truth *does* promise stability, it is because Hebrew tradition relies "on *covenant* as a means of establishing stable expectations in a changing world."[71]

The lyrics of the hymn "How Firm a Foundation" illustrates this beautifully: "How firm a foundation, ye Saints of the Lord, Is laid for your faith in his excellent word!"[72] The foundation is not firm because it is built upon some universal law or set of abstract principles. Rather, the foundation is firm because God has made us promises, and He keeps His promises. He will never forsake us, never abandon us in our hour of need. He will always be there to rescue us, support us, strengthen us, and sanctify us.

When we covenant with God, we do not know all that He might ask us to do. In His wisdom, He does not tell us beforehand what trials we will be called to endure, what responsibilities and stewardships we will be given, or what habits and lifestyles we will be asked to relinquish. In fact, as faithful disciples of Christ, our path may lead through "fiery trials," through sickness, health, poverty's vale, or abounding wealth. We just do not know. So it is not a very *safe* bet—but it is certainly a *good* one.

Reframing Our Questions: Chapter 5

Idea-truth: If I truly believe in God and strive to live the gospel with exactness, why don't I always get the blessings I expect or that were promised?

Person-truth: How can my hardships draw me closer to God and serve as a witness of His divine hand in my life?

The first question assumes that the gospel can be boiled down to a list of principles that, if carefully followed, grant us the blessings we seek from God. The question seems to presume that our relationship with God is more or less an economic one; that is, a relationship in which God has certain blessings that we desire and in order to get them from him we have to pay a certain price (i.e., obey certain commandments, etc.). While it may be true that God keeps His promises, His teachings might not be a recipe for worldly success or happiness. Unlike *idea*-truth, *person*-truth does not promise us knowledge or control of our futures. Instead, this approach suggests that what matters in life is coming to know God in personal and intimate ways, often through hardship and challenge—and, even, occasionally in the midst of God's silence.

CHAPTER 6

Knowing *person*-truth through covenant

The distinction between *idea*-truth and *person*-truth can help us understand the holy temple. The concept of "sacred" knowledge is foreign to the modern mind. This is because the *idea* view of truth prioritizes public observations and rational arguments. If truth is the same anywhere and everywhere, then it must be verified across multiple contexts by independent observers. For this reason, the *idea* view of truth can lead us to value observations and methods that are transparent, replicable, and accessible to public scrutiny. Truths that can be observed only by a select few (such as members of a particular research club, university department, or religious organization) will always be treated as suspect—perhaps even "cultish."

However, modern Latter-day Saint temple worship is quite at home with a *person* view of truth that focuses on covenants with God. In a relationship between two people, there is a level of intimacy that is acceptable only after they have pledged themselves in marriage. In the context of marriage, spouses can *know* each other more richly and intimately than they could as mere friends or acquaintances. In fact, the Old and New Testament sometimes uses the word *know* to refer to sexual intimacy (for example, Adam "knew" Eve). Spouses cannot *know* each other (in the most intimate sense) without first *covenanting* unconditional fidelity to each other.

We can use this as a metaphor for our relationship with God. We can come to know God in ways that are sacred and not (appropriately) open to public scrutiny. In fact, we must pledge ourselves to God before we can intimately *know* Him. When we make promises with God in the temple, for example, we enter into a covenant relationship with Him. Within that context, God can reveal Himself to us most fully. This can help us better understand the endowment ceremony. The rituals and ordinances performed in the temple are deeply rooted in Israelite tradition and custom.

The temple symbolizes our search for truth

When traveling through the wilderness, the Israelites constructed a tabernacle where they could perform the rituals of the Law of Moses. This tabernacle had an exterior courtyard that surrounded a tent in the middle. In the courtyard was the altar on which priests offered animal sacrifices. The tent in the middle was divided into two rooms by a veil. The first division was called the "Holy Place," and contained an altar on which the priests burnt sweet-smelling incense. On the other side of the dividing veil, in the "Holy of Holies" or "the Holiest Place," the Ark of the Covenant was placed, which represented the throne of God.[73]

Our modern temples have a similar architecture and follow the same symbolic pattern. When Adam and Eve were in the Garden of Eden, they walked and talked with God. When they transgressed God's commandment, they left God's presence. After we witness (and ritually reenact) the Creation and the Fall, we find ourselves on a symbolic journey back to God's presence, through stages: we leave the telestial world, enter into the terrestrial world, and then pass through the veil and into the celestial room of the temple. These three stages (telestial, terrestrial, and celestial) roughly correspond to the courtyard, Holy Place, and Holy of Holies in the ancient tabernacle.

This symbolic journey represents our reconciliation with God. We move from a life of sin to a life of righteous living (cleansed and redeemed by Christ). From there we enter into God's presence, where can converse with Him, learn from Him, and be with Him in the most personal and direct way possible. We are taught through symbols how to penetrate the veil as we approach His presence. The temple also teaches us about Christ, the plan of salvation, and the nature and possibilities of our relationship with God. While each of these teachings can be found in the scriptures, the temple adds further clarity.

However, all of this knowledge is guarded by sacred oaths and covenants. The layout and furnishings of the modern temple (and the Israelite tabernacle) reinforce this. The celestial room (or the Holy of Holies) represents full God's presence. To get there, we must pass altars (or places of promise-making). We cannot make that sacred approach without first *pledging* ourselves (and everything that we have) to God. Not only are these teachings protected by sacred covenants, we can only understand them through a lifetime of covenant keeping and of reenacting that symbolic approach to God's throne.

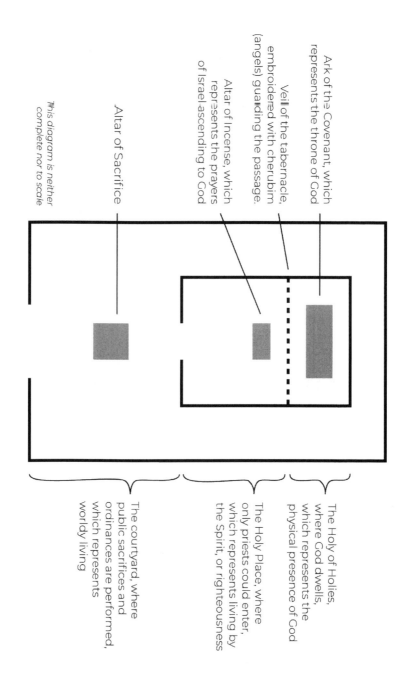

Ark of the Covenant, which represents the throne of God

Veil of the tabernacle, embroidered with cherubim (angels) guarding the passage.

Altar of Incense, which represents the prayers of Israel ascending to God

Altar of Sacrifice

This diagram is neither complete nor to scale

The Holy of Holies, where God dwells, which represents the physical presence of God

The Holy Place, where only priests could enter, which represents living by the Spirit, or righteousness

The courtyard, where public sacrifices and ordinances are performed, which represents worldly living

Sacred truth in scripture

In the scriptures, prophets occasionally experienced what we ritualize in the temple. Peter, James, John, Nephi, the brother of Jared, Moses, and others climbed mountains and spoke with God (or His messengers) face to face. They learned directly from the Truth Himself, so to speak. The temple is often referred to as the "mountain of the Lord," symbolizing these mountains of ancient times. These prophets then returned from the mountain with new understanding, a divine commission, and more knowledge than they could rightfully share with others. At least some of the knowledge they received from God in those encounters was *not* for public scrutiny.

For example, Peter, James, and John were led by Christ into a mountaintop, where they were visited in vision by Moses and Elias. Towards the end of the vision, the voice of God announced that Jesus was His Divine Son. We read, "And as they came down from the mountain, Jesus charged them, saying, Tell the vision to no man, until the Son of man be risen again from the dead" (John 17:9). Similarly, Nephi was led to the top of a very high mountain, where He saw a vision of the Christ's life, birth, death, and resurrection, as well as the events of the last days. Nephi wrote, "And behold, I, Nephi, am forbidden that I should write the remainder of the things which I saw and heard; wherefore the things which I have written sufficeth me; and I have written but a small part of the things which I saw" (1 Nephi 14:28).

In the book of Ether, we read that the brother of Jared climbed up the mount Shelem to ask God for help finding light for the barges he had built for his people. Christ showed Himself to the brother of Jared and talked with him face to face. Christ said: "Behold, thou shalt not suffer these things which ye have seen and heard to go forth unto the world, until the time cometh that I shall glorify my name in the flesh; wherefore, ye shall treasure up the things which ye have seen and heard, and show it to no man" (Ether 3:21). The brother of Jared saw many other great things but was commanded to "seal them up" (Ether 4:5) because "they shall not go forth unto the Gentiles until the day that they shall repent of their iniquity, and become clean before the Lord" (Ether 4:6).

Arriving at the destination

Each search for truth has a culminating finale, a destination. This differs depending on whether truth is a set of ideas or a person. Consider a well-known folk story about a Greek mathematician named Archimedes.[74] Archimedes discovered how to determine the volume of a complex object by immersing it in water and measuring displacement. As the story goes, he was sitting in the bath tub at the time of his discovery. He immediately jumped out and ran naked down the street, shouting ecstatically to all who could hear, "Eureka! Eureka!" which means, "I've found it! I've found it!" Archimedes was elated because he could grasp with his mind an abstract, mathematical law. His discovery was considered the product of his observation and ingenuity. He immediately shared his discovery with the world.

In the *person* view of truth, our pilgrimage back to God's presence takes place not just in our mind but rather in every aspect of our lives. We become *remade* as people through this journey. The culmination of this journey is ritualized in the endowment ceremony in our passage through the veil and into the celestial room. This ceremony foreshadows the most intimate and sacred communion with truth possible: the kind of personal encounter experienced by Moses as he spoke face-to-face with God on Mount

Sinai, or the similar experiences of Abraham, Enoch, Moroni, and others. The culminating moment is not an ecstatic, Archimedean "Eureka!" but a humbling, worshipful joy as we commune with our Father and are someday invited to dwell in His presence.

This experience is not a discovery but rather a *revelation*. It is not a product of our own ingenuity but a gift made possible through the grace of Christ. The peace and joy of such an experience transforms the whole person, and is not intended for public scrutiny (except, at times, at the behest of God). It is certainly not the sort of experience one runs naked down the street shouting about, as Archimedes did. This intimate way of knowing God can be as personal and private as our interactions with our spouse in the bedroom—protected and guarded by similar sacred obligations and duties, ritually undertaken by covenant.

Reframing Our Questions: Chapter 6

Idea-truth: If the sacred truths of the Holy Temple are really so important, why do we keep them a secret, rather than sharing them with everyone?

Person-truth: What must I do to prepare myself for the ritual communion with God that takes place in the Holy Temple, and how can I invite others to do the same?

The first question assumes that all truth should be verified in light of public scrutiny, whereas the second question assumes that our relationship with God can involve levels of familiarity and intimacy that are guarded by covenants. This kind of relational intimacy with God is not the sort of thing that one can have with abstract ideas. For this reason, the idea of "sacred truth," guarded by covenants, does not make as much sense from a conventional point of view, but makes perfect sense if we understand truth as a Person with whom we form a relationship.

CHAPTER 7

Our on-and-off relationship with *person*-truth

The *idea* and *person* views of truth can lead to different views on moral and societal progress. When we adopt an *idea* view of truth, we often assume that society is continually moving from antiquated ideals towards ever newer and better ones. We assume that knowledge is *cumulative*. Society, from this view, is on a fairly straightforward trajectory of continual progress. For many, the greatest intellectual or moral crime is to be "behind the times," "out of touch," or "on the wrong side of history."

Consider the popular computer game *Civilization*, originally developed by Sid Meier. In the game, the player shepherds a civilization from the stone age into the modern age. Part of the strategy of the game is deciding which technologies and social developments to prioritize while competing against neighboring nations. Within the game, no development is ever lost, once gained. Every new development builds upon previous developments, whether technological, social, or political.

Civilization is just a game, but it illustrates the assumption that progress is the inevitable result of collective human action. If truth is a set of ideas that we grasp with the mind, then all we must do is record those ideas in our collective memory. The invention of writing made this possible, and the information age makes this inevitable. From this view, as long as we can preserve some type of knowledge library we are unlikely to regress to earlier stages of development or forget the truth we have accumulated.

This is because the *idea* view of truth assumes that truth is discoverable by human methods and that truth is largely a matter of the mind. By archiving and cataloging discoveries and innovations in libraries and databanks, we maintain both their longevity and accessibility so they can never be truly forgotten. This applies to moral truth as well. From an *idea* view of truth, even if *individuals* engage in faulty moral reasoning, the moral beliefs of rational people across cultures and time will eventually converge. Changes in our collective moral reasoning are presumed to be almost always for the better.

This assumption sometimes leads to what C.S. Lewis termed "chronological snobbery," which is the "the uncritical acceptance of the intellectual climate common to our own age and the assumption that whatever has gone out of date is on that account discredited."[75] Figuring out the direction of progress only requires extrapolating current trends. From the *idea* view of truth, current societal consensus trumps the prior tradition, and *future* societal consensus trumps both. Only fools linger at the tail end of our onward march of social, moral, and intellectual progress. For example, as society starts to revisit and abandon the very concept of gender, this view might conclude that new consensus is informed by convergent moral reasoning, grounded in accumulated collective experience. We can treat the new consensus as more informed than the prior consensus, and the consensus of generations yet to come as more informed than both.

Our relationship with *person*-truth requires nurturing

As you may have guessed, *person*-truth treats moral progress very differently: our relationship with truth is inextricably connected to our relationship with God. Like any relationship, it must be *nurtured*. Without this nurturing, we may collectively lose our relationship with Truth, and reverse course in our spiritual progress (and wander in metaphorical foreign and desolate lands). Scripture contradicts the assumption that societal progress is inevitable or that knowledge inevitably increases over time. The Old Testament is thick with stories of apostasy, in which the Israelites neglected their covenants with God and slid backwards in their pilgrimage towards truth.

The prophet Jeremiah, for example, wrote: "The Lord said also unto me, ... Hast thou seen that which backsliding Israel hath done? she is gone up upon every high mountain and under every green tree, and there hath played the harlot. And I said after she had done all these things, Turn thou unto me. But she returned not" (Jeremiah 3:6-7). Notice the metaphor of *infidelity* that is used in these passages. Jeremiah continues, "Because my people hath forgotten me, they have burned incense to vanity, and they have caused them to stumble in their ways from the ancient paths, to walk in paths, in a way not cast up" (Jeremiah 18:15).

Similar themes are found in the Book of Mormon. Alma cried to the people of Ammonihah, "Behold, O ye wicked and perverse generation, how have ye forgotten the tradition of your fathers; yea, how soon ye have forgotten the commandments of God" (Alma 9:8). The prophet Mormon spoke of the Nephites who followed the wicked Amalickiah, "Thus we see how quick the children of men do forget the Lord their God, yea, how quick to do iniquity, and to be led away by the evil one" (Alma 46:8). The Nephites would often "forget the Lord their God" and "wax strong in iniquity" (Helaman 11:36). Later, the prophet Mormon wrote:

> And thus we can behold how *false*, and also the *unsteadiness* of the hearts of the children of men; yea, we can see that the Lord in his great infinite goodness doth bless and prosper those who put their trust in him. Yea, and we may see at the very time when he doth prosper his people, ... yea, then is the time that they do harden their hearts, and do *forget* the Lord their God, and do trample under their feet the Holy One—yea, and this because of their ease, and their exceedingly great prosperity.
>
> And thus we see that except the Lord doth chasten his people with many afflictions, yea, except he doth visit them with death and with terror, and with famine and with all manner of pestilence, *they will not remember him.* ... Yea, how quick to be lifted up in pride; yea, how quick to boast, and do all manner of that which is iniquity; and *how slow are they to remember* the Lord their God, and to give ear unto his counsels, yea, how slow to walk in wisdom's paths! Behold, they do not desire that the Lord their God, who hath created them, should rule and reign over them; notwithstanding his great goodness and his mercy towards them, they do set at naught his counsels, and they

will not that he should be their guide (Helaman 12:1-6; italics added).

Passages such as these permanently dispel the notion that society's moral trajectory is always upward and forward. In fact, it was when the Nephites and Lamanites exalted their own wisdom over the teachings of Christ and His servants that they faltered the most in their moral, societal, and spiritual progress.

None of this makes sense if truth is a set of universal principles, especially in a modern era where information can be so easily replicated, disseminated, and preserved. However, if truth is a *person*, then accumulated information is no guarantee of moral progress, and a photographic memory is no guarantee against moral regress. Our knowledge of truth is bound up with our covenantal relationship with God. We can lose truth as we neglect or betray that relationship. In the Book of Mormon, the Lord said:

> Blessed are those who hearken unto my precepts, and lend an ear unto my counsel, for they shall learn wisdom; for unto him that receiveth I will give more; and from them that shall say, We have enough, from them shall be taken away even that which they have (2 Nephi 28:30).

In other words, sin can lead us to lose—and even forget—knowledge we have previously had. We see this happen in human relationships all the time: people who are in love and then have a falling out will often forget the good times they've had together and only remember the bad. Sometimes, it is only when they've reconciled that they begin to remember the good times again. The same is true of our relationship with God: when we distance ourselves from Him, we can forget the times we have experienced His hand in our lives. We can forget the foundations of our relationship with God.

We progress on our journey by heeding God's voice

When we covenant our allegiance to Christ, He promises to lead us—both metaphorically and literally—safely through this "vale of sorrow into a far better land of promise" (Alma 37:45). He did this for the Israelites after they fled Egypt, Jared's people after they fled the city where the tower of Babel was being constructed,[76] Lehi's family after they fled Jerusalem,[77] and the Saints moving west after the death of the Prophet Joseph.[78]

Today, our (metaphorical) promised land is to build a global covenant community. This community is called Zion, a society in which God's laws are lived and normalized and in which residents walk and dwell in the presence of Divine Beings. In the Zion of Enoch's day, "the Lord came and dwelt with his people, and they dwelt in righteousness, ... [and] they were of one heart and one mind, and dwelt in righteousness; and there was no poor among them" (Moses 7:16, 18).

In the Nephite version of Zion, "they had all things common among them; therefore there were not rich and poor, bond and free, but they were all made free, and partakers of the heavenly gift ... and did walk after the commandments which they had received from their Lord and their God" (4 Nephi 1:3, 12). From a scriptural perspective, this is the pinnacle of societal and moral progress, and something towards which all disciples of Christ are striving.[79]

It is also worth noting that in each covenant journey through the wilderness, God sent directors to guide His covenant people safely through the dangers that plagued their journey. These have included pillars of fire, scriptures, liahonas, seer stones, prophets and apostles, and the Holy Spirit. A number of times, though, God's covenant people faltered in their progress. This always

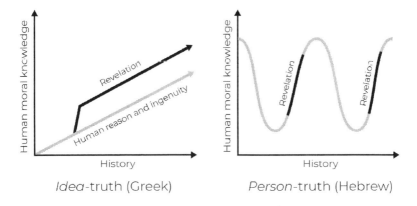

Idea-truth (Greek)   Person-truth (Hebrew)

happened when they neglected the instructions God had given to them through His conduits of revelation.

Alma taught his son Helaman about the Liahona (director, or compass) that the Lord provided to Lehi and his family. He wrote:

> It did work for them according to their faith in God; therefore, if they had faith to believe that God could cause that those spindles should point the way they should go, behold, it was done. ...
>
> Nevertheless ... they were slothful, and forgot to exercise their faith and diligence and then those marvelous works ceased, and they did not progress in their journey; Therefore, they tarried in the wilderness, or did not travel a direct course, and were afflicted with hunger and thirst, because of their transgressions (Alma 37:40-42).

Similarly, when the ancient Israelites disregarded the pleadings and guidance of Moses, they ended up living in the wilderness for forty years. Likewise, when the brother of Jared ceased to call upon God, he and his people tarried for years rather than progressing on their journey forward (Ether 2:13-14). In every case, progress was only made to the extent that people heeded the instructions of God within their covenant community. In *our* covenant community, the authorized channel of revelation includes the First Presidency, the Quorum of the Twelve Apostles, and the Holy Spirit.

From an *idea* view of truth, "societal progress" takes place independent of our relationship with God. We sometimes adopt this view in the Church. We assume that while societal progress is inevitable, it is also *slow*. Prophets "foresee" and "anticipate" future progress and can accelerate our progress. In this view, revelation allows Latter-day Saints to stay a little ahead of the moral and social progress curve, to be a "light on the hill," moving society forward with us.[80]

This may be why some Latter-day Saints become agitated and discouraged when it seems like leaders of the Church are straggling *behind* on this forward journey, or when prophets question the virtue of progressive changes taking place in society. When this happens, some assume that divine revelation is being hampered by tradition and unacknowledged prejudice. One former Latter-day Saint expressed this frustration: "The church, with its LGBT policies, is committing membership generational homicide. And it's a double-whammy for the LDS church, because as prophets, seers, and revelators, they are supposed to see AHEAD of the times."[81]

However, from a *person* view of truth, when we betray our covenants with God, we unhinge ourselves from the only Person who can keep us from faltering in our moral and spiritual progress. Our greatest concern should not be whether we are on the "right side of history," but whether we are on the right side of God.[82] We have been warned by apostles and prophets that society is heading in a direction that we really do not want to travel. When prophets warn against embracing the so-called "common sense" of our day, it is not because they are reluctant stragglers in society's march towards progress. Rather, it is because society may not actually be progressing at all on matters of greatest importance.

Reframing Our Questions: Chapter 7

Idea-truth: Why are modern prophets so often defending ideas that are so "old-fashioned" and behind the times, rather than being more responsive to emerging societal consensus (or even leading the way and getting ahead of the times)?

Person-truth: What sacred truths are being lost as we (as a society) neglect our relationship with God?

The first of these questions assumes that societal consensus will always point us in the direction of progress—as varying truth claims are subjected to public scrutiny, we inevitably discard discredited understandings in favor of newer and better understandings. The second question, however, assumes that our collective moral knowledge is contingent on our relationship with God. The closer and more intimate we are in our relationship with God (the Truth), the fuller and more discerning our understanding of what is right and true.

CHAPTER 8

What it means to be an authority on truth

How we think of truth influences on how we will think about *authority*. Questions about *who* can be an authority and *why* we trust them are answered very differently from a *person* view of truth than from an *idea* view of truth. From an *idea* view of truth, we assume that a person can only be an authority on subjects they have studied in a publicly replicable and verifiable way—and only insofar as their conclusions contribute to a converging consensus on the issues at hand.

Contrary to conventional wisdom, an appeal to authority is not always a logical fallacy, even from the perspective of *idea*-truth. A legitimate authority in the modern world, however, must meet two criteria:

1. He or she must have gained his or her expertise in a way that is publicly demonstrable and replicable by others. Others must be able to obtain the same expertise and arrive at the same conclusions (if they so desire).

2. The authority must contribute to a consensus of experts. If an expert's observations are open to public scrutiny, and his or her conclusions are replicable, a consensus of opinion will form.[83]

From this perspective, individuals are legitimate authorities if their truth claims are based on public observations that contribute to expert consensus.[84] Most scholarly dialogue relies on appeals to authority—scientists do not individually replicate every experiment done by their peers. Scholars assume that errant conclusions will eventually be corrected through replication, critical analysis, and consensus-building.

This is why, in the modern world, becoming an authority involves a process of peer-review, debate, and academic argument. Anyone brave enough is free to face the intellectual battlegrounds of the academic world. And anyone who is so brave, if they have enough wits about them, can become an authority (expert) in their area of research. No ordination, visitation, or special calling from God is required. One simply has to master the methods of scholarship and subject their work to public scrutiny.

From this perspective, prophets and apostles are *not* considered legitimate authorities, precisely because they do not meet the two criteria above. There is no transcript of Joseph Smith's conversation with the Father and the Son, and no known means to reproduce that sacred event. These observations cannot be guaranteed by the method Joseph employed. The same is true of today's Church leaders. The general public is seldom privy to their reasoning, their evidence, or their revelatory communications with God.

When seen in this light, it is perhaps not surprising that Hellenized (that is, Greek-influenced) Christianity came to rely so heavily on rational theology and consensus-seeking councils.[85] Indeed, many theologians seek to defend their sectarian traditions not with ongoing revelation, but with systematic logic and reason, in an attempt to build a consensus within their scholarly (or ecclesiastical) communities.[86]

Person-truth can commission messengers

If we think of truth as a *person*, someone can be an authority even if they cannot open their methods to public scrutiny—and even if they defy expert consensus. God (the Truth made Flesh) can visit and converse with specific persons in specific places and times and commission them to be His spokesmen and to share His teachings. From this view, while these visitations and conversations may not be open to public scrutiny, prophets and apostles can still be considered *authorities.*

Faulconer has noted that, as Latter-day Saints, "We dare to say that God continues to reveal himself authoritatively to human beings through another human being."[87] And, similarly, Elder Jeffrey R. Holland has taught, "It is no trivial matter for this Church to declare to the world prophecy, seership, and revelation, but we do declare it."[88] *Idea*-truth cannot have spokesmen. But the Truth made Flesh (Christ) *can.* He can declare His word through spokesmen chosen at His discretion, usually through no merits of their own (such as, for example, Enoch, Moses, or Saul).

From this perspective, to become such an authority on *person*-truth requires that we are called of God. In the Articles of Faith, we read: "We believe that a man must be called of God, by prophecy, and by the laying on of hands by those who are in authority, to preach the Gospel and administer in the ordinances thereof" (AoF 1:5). Nothing we do on our own volition can make us such an authority on *person*-truth because it has little to do with scholarly methods (replicable or otherwise). In the Doctrine and Covenants, the Lord refers to His servants as the "weak things of the world" (D&C 1:19).[89]

The concept of prophets are deeply rooted in Hebrew tradition. The Hebrews, after all, were identified by their lineage from the prophets Abraham, Isaac, and Jacob. They were led through the wilderness by the prophet Moses. They gave us the writings of Samuel, Isaiah, Jeremiah, and other prophets of the Old Testament. We read in the Old Testament that the Lord "testified against Israel, and against Judah, by all the prophets, and by all the seers, saying, Turn ye from your evil ways, and keep my commandments and my statutes, according to all the law which I commanded your fathers, and which I sent to you by my servants the prophets" (2 Kings 17:13).

Simply put, a prophet is someone appointed by the Truth Himself to speak *for* the truth—and is quite literally a "truth-teller." As Truman G. Madsen noted, prophets are not merely "fore-tellers," they are also "'forth-tellers,' meaning that they speak forth boldly in judgment and in recommendation as to their own time."[90] Indeed, the Greek word *prophetes* (προφάτης) used in the New Testament means "forth speaker." Similarly, the Old Testament Hebrew word *nabiy* (אִיבֶנָ) means something very much like "spokesman."

In the previous chapter, we explained that in the *person* view of truth, society will not always take a forward trajectory of moral progress. In fact, if societal consensus is not informed (to some degree) by contemporary messengers from God, it will likely be wrong. For this reason, Christ's servants will often contradict expert consensus. We cannot dismiss the counsel of prophets as just "good advice" to be measured against the conventional wisdom of our times.

The *idea* view of truth can quietly sneak into the way we think about prophets. From this view, it is not who speaks that matters, but *what* is said. Someone is a prophet if they teach universal truth, regardless of their divine commission. In other words, if President Monson teaches truth, then he is a prophet. But *so is the Dalai Lama, if he teaches the same* truth. From the *idea* view, the *content* of their teaching matters most. This is why, from the *idea* view of truth, prophets are only authorities if they contribute to an ongoing consensus.

From a *person* view of truth, however, we are equally concerned about the divine authority of the speaker. In this view, *who* is speaking is just as important as *what* is being said. The *source* matters as much as the *content*. We see the *person* view expressed in the temple drama. After they were driven out of the Garden of Eden, Adam and Eve did not search for abstract "truth." Rather, they sought and waited for *authorized messengers*. To us, this is a crucial distinction: their concern was about the source of what they were taught, and not merely the content.

The Holy Ghost confirms the divine commission of prophets

The divine commission of a prophet is established differently than the authority of secular scholars and experts. Prophets generally do not have a diploma that establishes their divine stewardship, and there is no (mortal) third-party accrediting agency that verifies their authority. Rather, we must seek personal revelation from God to know whether they are genuine prophets and apostles. From an *idea* view of truth, the Holy Ghost merely confirms whether the ideas taught are "truth." But from a *person* view of truth, the Holy Ghost affirms the stewardship of the person teaching the truths.

Seeking personal revelation from God to confirm the divine stewardship of His servants is a kind of "independent verification" that is vastly different from the peer review processes valued by Western thought. When we engage in such prayer and seek such confirmations, we are not comparing the teachings of the prophets against scholarly consensus, nor are we examining their methods and replicating their reasoning. We are instead asking a simple question of God: "Are these men commissioned by you? Are they indeed prophets and messengers with a divine calling?" Brigham Young famously said:

> What a pity it would be if we were lead by one man to utter destruction! Are you afraid of this? I am *more* afraid that this people have so much confidence in their leaders that they will not inquire for themselves of God whether they are lead by him. ... Let every man and woman know, by the whispering of the Spirit of God to themselves whether their leaders are walking in the path the Lord dictates or not.[91]

Some have misread this statement and think Brigham Young feared that people could be led astray unless they independently verify each of his instructions. However, when read in context, Brigham Young was mimicking what *others* (nonbelievers) had said about the Saints. He does *not* share the fears held by nonbelievers, he says, but instead fears that people will not heed the teachings of the prophets with the conviction that comes the Spirit of God.

Joseph Smith wrote, "A prophet is a prophet only when he was acting as such."[92] Some interpret this to mean that a prophet is only a prophet if he is teaching what can be objectively recognized as truth. This adopts the central assumptions of the *idea* view of truth. But from a *person* view of truth, Joseph Smith was merely stating that prophets are not on the Lord's errand every minute of every day—not that we need to independently verify everything they teach before heeding their warnings and instructions.

None of this should be misinterpreted to imply that prophets are infallible, or never make mistakes. As President Dieter F. Uchtdorf taught, "There have been times when members or leaders in the Church have simply made mistakes. There may have been things said or done that were not in harmony with our values, principles, or doctrine."[93] Rather, from a *person* view of truth, prophets can have a divine commission while also being mortal, imperfect people. King Benjamin expresses this perspective clearly:

> I have not commanded you to come up hither to trifle with the words which I shall speak, but that you should hearken unto me, and open your ears that ye may hear, and your hearts that ye may understand, and your minds that the mysteries of God may be unfolded to your view. I have not commanded you to come up hither that ye should fear me or that ye should think that I of myself am more than a mortal man. But I am like as yourselves, subject to all manner of infirmities in body and mind; yet I have been chosen by this people, and consecrated by my father, and was suffered by the hand of the Lord that I should be a ruler and a king over this people (Mosiah 2:9-11).

Here, King Benjaming says three things: (1) People should not fear him as they might fear God, because he is a mortal man, subject to imperfection. (2) People should not trifle with his words but should open their ears and hearts to what he has to say. (3) He has a divine commission from the people and from God to be their teacher. This is what it means to treat prophets as authorities (from the *person* view of truth): we recognize their mortal fallibility, but we do not trifle with their words. Conversely, recognizing the dangers of trifling with their words is *not* the same thing as denying their mortality or fallibility.

Inspired leadership does not require uniform consistency

One implication of *idea*-truth is that the actions of divinely inspired leaders will be consistent across time. After all, if truth is a universal, timeless, unchangeable set of ideas, then actions based in truth will converge towards the same decisions when confronted with the same set of facts. From this view, just as with physical laws of nature, if you have the exact same starting conditions, you will observe the same results. Any deviation would imply that we have not yet found the fundamental truth of the matter (or that there are undetected differences in the initial conditions).

For example, from an *idea*-truth perspective, if two individuals commit the same serious sin, and each confesses to his or her bishop, the two bishops will be expected to give the same counsel and administer the same ecclesiastical discipline. If they do not, we might assume that one or both bishops are not acting under divine inspiration.

Now, someone might (rightly) argue that the two individuals have different life trajectories and experiences, and do not *need* the same response from their bishops. So, let's change the scenario to involve the *same* individual, but in two parallel realities that are identical in every other respect. If the two bishops are both divinely inspired, would we not expect the same response from each bishop? *Idea*-truth implies that deviations in the face of identical conditions means that at least one of the bishops has got something wrong.

Similarly, we might assume that if God inspires the actions of President Russell M. Nelson, then President Nelson is doing the exact same things that President Gordon B. Hinkley would have done in the same contexts, or that President Dallin H. Oaks would have done were *he* president of the Church instead. We assume that because prophets act with divine authority, their leadership would be the same.

For this reason, when we see the personalities of individual prophets filter into their decisions, we assume that those aspects of their leadership are *not* divinely inspired. When we see the personalities and dispositions of individual bishops filter into their ecclesiastical leadership and spiritual counsel, we assume that— to a significant extent—they are *also* not divinely inspired. We sometimes hear members talk about "leadership roulette," or "bishop roulette," a term that implies that what happens when you seek counsel and confess to your bishop depends as much on the bishop as it does on the specific details of your situation.

This sort of thinking assumes that there is a single right course of action for any given context, and that inspired individuals will converge on that course of action. But this is a very *Greek* assumption. Hebrew thought does not require this assumption at all. *Person*-truth (through the Holy Spirit) can reside with us in the individual contexts of our lives, and this does not mean that there is only one course of action that the Holy Spirit will ratify. For example, we might feel prompted to comfort a friend, but *what that looks like* will depend on our personality, experience, and culture.

The same is true for ecclesiastical action. If someone visits his or her bishop and confesses serious sins, it may be that disfellowship, probation, and no action are all potentially good paths forward. What looks to some like "random variation" in ecclesiastical response may be myriads of inspired leaders all pursuing different right answers to the same questions. Similarly, other hypothetical presidents of the Church might have made different leadership decisions than President Nelson, but this does not mean that President Nelson is acting with any less divine authority.

God calls mortal people into positions of leadership with different personalities and inclinations, and He allows those personalities and inclinations to shape their service. That is by divine design. It is only from an *idea*-truth perspective (which its Greek emphasis on sameness across contexts) that we take issue with the idea that different leaders can make different inspired decisions in response to the same conditions. From a Hebrew perspective, we can embrace that difference without attributing all of it to fallibility (although, as described earlier, there is certainly some of that too). We can embrace the *particularity* of divine truth in our lives, our stewardships, and our communities.

Reframing Our Questions: Chapter 8

Idea-truth: Who was right and who was wrong: President Brigham Young or President Russell M. Nelson? (Assuming, of course, there is some point of disagreement between them.)

Person-truth: Who has been commissioned by God to lead His church at this time?

The first question assumes that because truth is an abstract and unchanging idea (the same in all places and at all times), if two prophets give different instructions, then one of them must be wrong. In contrast, the second question relinquishes the need to determine which instructions are based in unchangeable doctrine. In this view, the task before us is to accept that a living God actively chooses and authorizes particular leaders at particular times for His own divine purposes.

Idea-truth: How can prophets be divine messengers if they teach in ways that reflect the norms and assumptions of their particular culture?

Person-truth: How can prophets guide us through the particulars of our social, historical, cultural, or political context?

Idea-truth assumes that if a prophet's teachings seem to reflect their cultural assumptions, they—by virtue of that fact—cannot also be divine instructions. For example, if prior prophets emphasized dress or grooming practices that are not universally applicable, we might be inclined to dismiss their teachings on the subject as the precepts of men rather than of God. However, *person*-truth assumes that prophetic teachings can be divinely inspired even if they are not applicable across all times or cultures. We need not dismiss as error prophetic teachings and warnings to Saints of other generations, who were living in different historical and cultural contexts than our own and therefore faced different spiritual dangers than we do.

CHAPTER 9

The archnemesis of *person*-truth

From the *idea* view of truth, falsehood shares many of the same attributes as truth, but there are also differences. While falsehood is not universal or unchangeable, it *does* consist of a series of passive ideas. Like truth, falsehood is a matter of the mind. We develop false ideas when we engage in bad reasoning or when we draw false conclusions from our observations. We can also invent false ideas in order to deceive others (in contrast, truth cannot be invented, only discovered). However, from the *idea* view of truth, we are dealing with *ideas*—whether those ideas are true or false.

If we take the *person* view of truth seriously, though, we also change our view of falsehood. The great battle in this life is not between truth and falsehood, but Truth and Falsehood. *Person*-truth has an enemy, the father of lies. Lucifer (known to us as Satan), the devil, personifies falsehood and deception just as surely as God personifies truth. In other words, we might say that there is a *person*-falsehood as well.

President James E. Faust explained, "As the great deceiver,

Lucifer has marvelous powers of deception."[94] Paul wrote to the Corinthians, "And no marvel; for Satan himself is transformed into an angel of light" (2 Corinthians 11:14). In the Book of Mormon, Jacob taught that the devil was that "being who beguiled our first parents, who transformeth himself nigh unto an angel of light, and stirreth up the children of men unto secret combinations of murder and all manner of secret works of darkness" (2 Nephi 9:9).

From this view, the great question is not, "What is truth?" Instead, the great question is, "*Who* is truth?" Other questions might be, "Who *speaks* for truth?" or "Is this a message from Truth or His enemy?" Our great task is not to sort between true and false ideas but to learn to discern the voice of Truth and the disguises of His enemy. In different words, the question is not *what to believe*, but *who to follow*. Alma taught:

> Behold, I say unto you, that the good shepherd doth call you; yea, and in his own name he doth call you, which is the name of Christ ... And now if ye are not the sheep of the good shepherd, of what fold are ye? Behold, I say unto you, that the devil is your shepherd, and ye are of his fold ...
>
> For I say unto you that whatsoever is good cometh from God, and whatsoever is evil cometh from the devil. Therefore, if a man bringeth forth good works he hearkeneth unto the voice of the good shepherd, and he doth follow him; but whosoever bringeth forth evil works, the same becometh a child of the devil, for he hearkeneth unto his voice, and doth follow him (Alma 5:38-41).

In these verses, the great choice is not between two different sets of doctrines or beliefs but between two different *masters*.

The opposite of *person*-truth is also active

From the *person* view of truth, Truth is active in the world (as opposed to an abstract idea awaiting discovery). But so is the father of lies. He is actively trying to deceive us and lead us away from the Truth made Flesh. For example, Adam and Eve did not fall prey to errors of reason or mistaken observations—they were actively deceived by the devil. While the *person* view makes truth more personal and real, it can also make its opposite more dangerous. False ideas cannot come looking for us or actively keep us prisoner. But Falsehood can.

Those who lead people away from Christ are not *always* merely mistaken in their beliefs. Korihor, known by readers of the Book of Mormon as an anti-Christ, described his own experiences:

> But behold, the devil hath deceived me; for he appeared unto me in the form of an angel, and said unto me: Go and reclaim this people, for they have all gone astray after an unknown God. And he said unto me: There is no God; yea, and he taught me that which I should say. And I have taught his words; and I taught them because they were pleasing unto the carnal mind; and I taught them, even until I had much success, insomuch that I verily believed that they were true; and for this cause I withstood the truth (Alma 30:53).

From Korihor's experience, we learn that just as Truth can commission messengers, so can His enemy. The father of lies has agents working in the world, sowing seeds of confusion and deception. Bad reasoning or errant observations (falsehood in the world of *idea*-truth) cannot do this.

From the *idea* view of truth, there are no false ideas that we cannot think our way out of. We can always revise our ideas based on systematic observation and rational analysis, no matter how wrong they were to start with. But if there really is a person who personifies falsehood and spreads lies, this may not be the case. In the Book of Mormon, Lehi had a dream about our journey to Christ (Truth). He observed "mists of darkness" that made it difficult to see the way. We read, "And the mists of darkness are the temptations of the devil, which blindeth the eyes, and hardeneth the hearts of the children of men, and leadeth them away into broad roads, that they perish and are lost" (1 Nephi 12:17).

In other words, there may really be intellectual snares and traps that, once sprung, we cannot *think* our way out of. It is possible, from this view, to be held captive by a lie or *possessed* by a false view of the world. Mormon tells us that at one point, "Satan did go about, leading away the hearts of the people" and that "thus did Satan get possession of the hearts of the people again, insomuch that he did blind their eyes" (3 Nephi 2:2-3). When this happens, everything we see is filtered through the lie. Even our questions become distorted by the false premises that have captured our minds, which is part of the trap.

From an *idea* view of truth, the proper treatment for this would be good rational counterarguments. But from a *person* view of truth, rational arguments may be insufficient. Divine *rescue* is often needed. This can involve the Holy Spirit, the scriptures, prayer, and even priesthood authority. When Satan visited Moses and attempted to deceive him, Moses could not get him to go away using his own authority or reasoning. He had to invoke the name of *Christ* and draw upon *His* power and authority (see Moses 1:12-22). The word of Christ (the Truth made Flesh) can pierce the deceptions of the adversary and illuminate our minds through His presence. Mormon taught,

Whosoever will may lay hold upon the word of God, which is quick and powerful, which shall divide asunder all the cunning and the snares and the wiles of the devil, and lead the man of Christ in a strait and narrow course across that everlasting gulf of misery which is prepared to engulf the wicked—

And land their souls, yea, their immortal souls, at the right hand of God in the kingdom of heaven, to sit down with Abraham, and Isaac, and with Jacob, and with all our holy fathers, to go no more out (Helaman 3:29-30).

Some members (and former members) criticize Church leaders for discouraging members from reading anti-Mormon or ex-Mormon literature. From their view, those who love truth should never be afraid of competing ideas. False ideas, from this view, cannot hurt us. Nothing requires us to believe what we read, so it cannot ever hurt to be exposed to new ways of looking at the world.

However, if we adopt a *person* view of truth, we see things differently. It *is* possible for false ideas to hurt us. It *is* possible for the adversary to ensnare us with deception, even if our explorations are innocently motivated. This is why President James E. Faust warned, "It is not good practice to become intrigued by Satan and his mysteries. No good can come from getting close to evil. Like playing with fire, it is too easy to get burned."[95]

The opposite of *person*-truth uses *false* covenants

Just as our pilgrimage toward *person*-truth is grounded in covenants with God, the servants of Falsehood also (sometimes) make covenants with *their* master (the adversary). It is possible to *literally* make a deal with the devil. The first recorded example is found in the story of Cain. We read:

And it came to pass that Cain took one of his brothers' daughters to wife, and they loved Satan more than God.

And Satan said unto Cain: Swear unto me by thy throat, and if thou tell it thou shalt die; and swear thy brethren by their heads, and by the living God, that they tell it not; for if they tell it, they shall surely die; and this that thy father may not know it; and this day I will deliver thy brother Abel into thine hands.

And Satan sware unto Cain that he would do according to his commands. And all these things were done in secret (Moses 5:28-30).

Unlike the Truth made Flesh (Christ), however, the father of lies does not keep his promises. We read, "The devil will not support his children at the last day, but doth speedily drag them down to hell" (Alma 30:60). But this does not keep people from making pacts with the adversary. In the Book of Mormon, we read about evil men who formed *secret combinations:* "And they did enter into a covenant one with another, yea, even into that covenant which was given by them of old, which covenant was given and administered by the devil, to combine against all righteousness" (3 Nephi 6:28).

Another group "formed a secret combination, even as they of old; which combination is most abominable and wicked above all, in the sight of God" (Ether 8:18). Moroni explains:

And now I, Moroni, do not write the manner of their oaths and combinations, for it hath been made known unto me that they are had among all people, and they are had among the Lamanites.

And they have caused the destruction of this people of whom I am now speaking, and also the destruction of the people of Nephi.

And whatsoever nation shall uphold such secret combinations, to get power and gain, until they shall spread over the nation, behold, they shall be destroyed; for the Lord will not suffer that the blood of his saints, which shall be shed by them, shall always cry unto him from the ground for vengeance upon them and yet he avenge them not (Ether 8:20-22).

In short, Truth's archnemesis is also a master counterfeiter. He mimics Truth and His ways, while striving to deceive us into abandoning our covenants with Truth. He does this in part by mimicking covenants themselves. He will at times invite his chief followers to make similar pacts, but instead of pacts that hold us accountable before God and to serve our fellow man, they are pacts of sin and deception.

Reframing Our Questions: Chapter 9

Idea-truth: How can we convince someone who has been led astray by false ideas of the error of their beliefs and doctrinal understandings?

Person-truth: How can we invite someone who has been (or is being) led astray to obtain spiritual and intellectual confirmations through personal experiences with God?

From the perspective of *idea*-truth, it is necessary to "think one's way through" false beliefs using the tools of rational analysis and systematic observation. Rational analysis is always encouraged, but *person*-truth does not always see it as sufficient. It is possible to get caught in rational traps that have no escape without intervention from Truth Himself. The enemy of Truth—Falsehood—is also dynamic and active, and just as willing to appeal to our reason and loyalty. Countering darkness and error often requires more than rational persuasion. It requires us to invite others to seek deeper and more meaningful experiences with God, and to step into greater personal relationship with the living Truth by making and keeping covenants, and seeking help from divinely chosen servants.

CHAPTER 10

What is sin, if truth is a person?

The way we think about truth changes how we think about sin. From the *idea* view of truth, moral truth is a set of universal rules or principles. From this view, an action is wrong when it violates abstract moral truth. To be a good person means to comply with the dictates of these abstract laws. Most importantly, these standards must be universal and unchanging. As Richards and O'Brien note:

> [Most of us assume that] rules (in the form of laws) must apply 100 percent of the time; otherwise, the rule is "broken." Likewise, rules (in the form of promises) apply to 100 percent of the people involved and apply equally; otherwise, we consider the rule to be unfair. Since God is both reliable and fair, surely his rules must apply equally to all people. Natural laws, like gravity, are no respecters of persons, after all. When we cannot determine how to apply

a biblical law or promise to everyone, we declare it to be "cultural" and thus flexible in application.[96]

In other words, from the *idea* view of truth, for an act be *truly* and *ultimately* wrong, the moral code that forbids it must not depend on context. Local or situated moral codes might deem an act inappropriate or imprudent, but they cannot define an act as truly evil because they vary across time and space. Only a *universal* (that is, fixed, immutable, or absolute) moral code can do that. From the *idea* view of truth, if we demonstrate that a moral precept is unique to a particular place and time (rather than universal), we can regard it as a human invention.

The philosopher Immanuel Kant's concept of the *categorical imperative* is an example of this sort of thinking. Kant reasoned that the most fundamental moral dictate (i.e., the "categorical imperative") was to "act only according to that maxim whereby you can, at the same time, will that it should become a universal law."[97] Other moral philosophers have sampled the moral intuitions and ethical traditions of cultures around the world (and in history) and have attempted to discover norms that seem to be *universal* across cultures and times.[98]

From the *idea* view of truth, our ability to live a moral life is as much an indication of our intelligence or philosophical intuition as it is our receptivity to God. The smarter we are, the more we can discern which rules are more universal or fundamental than others (and, conversely, which are less important by virtue of being contextual). When seen in this light, the Holy Spirit becomes a sort of teaching assistant or celestial tutor, someone who helps us figure out universal truth. Like any student, from this perspective our goal is to eventually learn the eternal "moral mathematics" so thoroughly that we have no further need for the instructor.

Sin is a damaged relationship with God

In contrast, from a *person* view of truth, sin is less about whether our behaviors comply with some universal moral code and more about our relational stance toward God and our fellow man. When we are righteous, it is *not* because we have meticulously complied with the patterns of behavior prescribed by some abstract law. From the *person* view of truth, we are righteous because we have formed a saving relationship with Christ. As Richards and O'Brien note, "in contrast to the modern Western worldview, in ancient worldviews it went without saying that relationships (not rules) define reality."[99]

Seen this way, sin is a sickness in our relationships. By definition, when we treat others with enmity and malice, we become spiritually separated from them. Similarly, when we rebel against God, we are no longer in harmony with His will. We enter into a state of continuing conflict with Him. President Ezra Taft Benson famously taught, "The central feature of pride is enmity—enmity toward God and enmity toward our fellowmen. Enmity means 'hatred toward, hostility to, or a state of opposition.'"[100] He continued, "Pride is the universal sin, the great vice."[101] Conversely, righteousness is more than just compliance with universal laws; righteousness is closeness to and unity with God.

An example may help illustrate the difference. Imagine that your friend lied to you about something that was important to you. You feel that your trust has been betrayed, and as a consequence your friendship is strained. Later, your friend approaches you and says, "Hey, I just wanted to say that I've been learning a lot about universal truth, and I realize now that there is a moral rule against lying. I'm sorry for breaking that law, it was wrong of me to do." Would this apology restore your trust and repair your friendship? Perhaps a little.

But consider an alternative scenario where your friend approaches you and says, "Hey, I just wanted to say that I now recognize how much my actions have hurt you. You valued your trust in me, and I violated that. I feel that my actions have alienated us from each other. What can I do to restore our friendship?" When compared to the first approach, this seems much more personal and sincere. This is because what makes lying wrong has less to do with some abstract law and more to do with how it damages relationships. The same is true in our relationship with God. Sin is wrong not because it violates some abstract rule, but because it alienates us from our Creator.

The scriptures are clear that complying with moral rules cannot save or redeem us without a covenant relationship with God. Without a genuine relationship with Christ, none of our "good acts" are counted as righteousness to us (nor can they save us). The Book of Mormon teaches "that salvation doth not come by the law alone" (Mosiah 13:28) and that the Anti-Nephi-Lehites "did not suppose that salvation came by the law of Moses; but the law of Moses did serve to strengthen their faith in Christ" (Alma 25:16). Likewise, Jacob taught his people, "for this intent we keep the law of Moses, it pointing our souls to [Christ]" (Jacob 4:5).

Within a *person* view of truth, it is to God that we are ultimately accountable, not to some faceless, abstract law. We will never "face" an abstract principle to account for our deeds, but we *will* face God. As the prophet Moroni declared:

> In that great day when ye shall be brought to stand before the Lamb of God—then will ye say that there is no God? ... Do ye suppose that ye shall dwell with him under

a consciousness of your guilt? Do ye suppose that ye could be happy to dwell with that holy Being, when your souls are racked with a consciousness of guilt that ye have ever abused his laws? (Mormon 9:2-3).

It is not because we violated impersonal law that we will feel guilt, but because we violated *His* laws. It is not an abstract *idea* we have flouted, but a *person* we have resisted and wronged. And it is that the concrete presence of that person that will bring to remembrance all our guilt. Moroni further warned the wicked of the coming day in which they "shall be brought to see [their] nakedness before God," at which time their impending separation from God will "kindle a flame of unquenchable fire" upon them (Mormon 9:5).

We must know God's will within our context

From a *person* view of truth, what Elder McConkie says about Christ—that is, that He stands revealed or remains forever unknown—applies also to the moral precepts He wishes us to follow. Moral law cannot be reduced to a series of universal absolutes, and especially not the kind that are discovered by rational or empirical analysis. It may be possible to deduce specific facts about any specific triangle based on abstract geometric laws—but it is *not* possible to deduce every right action in any given context using some sort of moral calculus. Because *person*-truth exists within our context, we cannot know beforehand all the things we should do at any given time.

This is not to say that there aren't commitments we make that we carry into every context and situation. For example, we can say that adultery is wrong both here and now *and* there and then. Further, we can commit to never violate this divine law so long as we live. But there is also room to believe that *context* matters—if a woman were to willingly sleep with someone other than her husband to save the lives of innocent hostages he has threatened, we cannot judge her as having done a moral wrong. Moral reasoning cannot offer the right course of action prior to every conceivable context.

Nephi, for example, could never have navigated his encounter with drunken Laban without the "in-the-moment" guidance of the Holy Spirit, no matter how much prior philosophical, moral, or religious training he had. As Nephi recounts:

> And it came to pass that I was constrained by the Spirit that I should kill Laban; but I said in my heart: Never at any time have I shed the blood of man. And I shrunk and would that I might not slay him. ...
>
> And it came to pass that the Spirit said unto me again: Slay him, for the Lord hath delivered him into thy hands; Behold the Lord slayeth the wicked to bring forth his righteous purposes. It is better that one man should perish than that a nation should dwindle and perish in unbelief. ...
>
> Therefore I did obey the voice of the Spirit, and took Laban by the hair of the head, and I smote off his head with his own sword (1 Nephi 4:10-18).

There is simply no moral calculus that could have led Nephi to the same conclusions without in-the-moment, specific guidance from God. Most of us instinctively recognize this. This is why none of us attempt this sort of moral math on our own. If Nephi had arrived at the same conclusions through rational analysis alone, we would believe that he had rationalized murder. It was not the *reasons given* that made his action the right thing to do—it was the voice of the Spirit (or, in other words, Truth personified). We can think of the Holy Ghost as more than an instructor teaching us abstract principles. Rather, the Holy Ghost is how the Truth (God) can *be with us in our varying contexts.* He helps us see what can only be seen within the context of action, no matter how much we analyze the issues ahead of time.

Nephi concludes his sacred record by exhorting us with these words: "For behold, again I say unto you that if ye will enter in by the way, and receive the Holy Ghost, it will show unto you all things what ye should do" (2 Nephi 32:5). Later, we read of Alma teaching his son Helaman, "Counsel with the Lord in all thy doings, and he will direct thee for good" (Alma 37:37). In Proverbs we read, "Trust in the Lord with all thine heart; and lean not unto thine own understanding. In all thy ways acknowledge him, and he shall direct thy paths" (Proverbs 3:5-6). The decisions we face can be seen rightly only when our minds are illuminated by the Spirit of Christ, who is the Truth made flesh.

From this view, the number of things that can alienate us from God increases tremendously. No longer is there a unchangeable list of "dos" and "don'ts," or "Thou Shalts" and "Thou Shalt Nots." Rather, almost *anything* (no matter how innocuous) could be sin, if the Holy Spirit prompts us to do otherwise. As King Benjamin said, "I cannot tell you all the things whereby ye may commit sin; for there are divers ways and means, even so many that I cannot number them" (Mosiah 4:29). But conversely, there are also an infinite number of otherwise mundane acts that can be counted to us for righteousness. When the Holy Spirit prompts us to call a friend, or write a letter, or to read a book, those actions *become* the right thing to do, even if they were morally neutral before.

Reframing Our Questions: Chapter 10

Idea-truth: What universal laws have I violated when I sin?

Person-truth: How have my actions wronged God and others? How have I violated sacred covenants with God?

While it is sometimes fruitful to generalize from God's commandments, it is not always helpful. Sometimes commandments are context-specific and based in covenants. *Person*-truth does not need to derive such instructions from universal rules in order to treat them as divinely inspired. The litmus test for divine truth is not *universality*, but divine *origin*. Instructions that are specific to our particular culture and sociohistorical context are not treated as less divine or important because they are not universal. Furthermore, *Person*-truth treats sin as a slight against God, not against an abstract rule—and so the goal of repentance is to restore our relationship with God.

Idea-truth: What abstract rules do I need to live by to be a good person?

Person-truth: How can I carry the Holy Spirit with me into every context, to help me enact God's will for me in my day-to-day life?

When we treat "being good" as a series of behavioral checklists, or a series of rules to follow, we may be operating from an *idea*-truth perspective. From a *person*-truth perspective, being good is less about following rules and more about developing a relationship with God. Abstract rules are useful generalizations, but our ultimate goal is to bring the Holy Spirit with us into our life situations and receive ongoing, personal guidance from God. This should not justify violating sacred covenants (e.g., the claim, "the law of chastity is a guideline, not a hard and fast rule," should be rightly treated as a selfish rationalization). Rather, it means that we cannot assume that we are sufficiently good merely because we follow abstract rules—we need a relationship with Christ and the ongoing guidance of the Holy Ghost.

CHAPTER 11

Rethinking the Atonement of Christ

How we think about truth (and how we think about sin) influences how we think about Christ's sacrifice for us. We feel it necessary, however, to begin this chapter with an important caveat from C.S. Lewis:

> We are told that Christ was killed for us, that His death has washed out our sins, and that by dying He disabled death itself. ... Any theories we build up as to how Christ's death did all this are, in my view, quite secondary: mere plans or diagrams to be left alone if they do not help us, and, even if they do help us, not to be confused with the thing itself.[102]

Every committed Christian accepts that Christ's death can save us. But there are many different theories about *how* this happens, and *why* Christ's death was necessary. The scriptures do not give technical explanations of the Atonement. Rather, they use metaphors instead. They compare sin and forgiveness to birth, food, medicine, money, lost livestock, marriage, government, and other things. These metaphors each reveal important insights into the Atonement, and each potentially conceals important insights as well.

One of the more common conceptions of the Atonement is commonly called the *Penal-Substitution* theory of the Atonement.[103] The essence of the penal-substitution theory is, as C.S. Lewis succinctly states it, "being let off because Christ has volunteered to bear a punishment instead of us."[104] This view assumes that sin is the violation of an abstract moral law. This abstract moral law requires that a penalty be exacted for sin, typically in the form of personal suffering (such as the fiery damnation of hell, or an afflicted conscience).

From this view, God is a preeminent legal scholar and well-versed in cosmic law. He sees a loophole that allows Him to save His sinning children: *vicarious* punishment. It will only work if the punishment is voluntarily accepted by one who has not also violated the law (such as the sinless Christ). On this view, because Jesus was perfectly sinless, He could stand as a worthy substitute for us. In suffering on our behalf a punishment that He does not deserve—but which *we* most certainly do—He is able to satisfy the demands of cosmic Justice.

If we meet the new conditions that God and His Son now set for us, it becomes possible for us to escape damnation and be "let off the hook," so to speak. The new conditions are much more generous, since Christ can exercise much more discretion than the inflexible demands of universal law. In this way, God can extend to us mercy while satisfying justice, and be simultaneously both just and merciful. This view of the Atonement draws heavily from the *idea* view of truth, because it conceptualizes sin as the violation of the abstract law. It treats Christ's death and suffering as required by that same law (which God cannot override).

Person-truth and the Atonement

If we understand sin as a way of living that alienates us from God, rather than as a violation of immutable, abstract law, this can change how we think of the Atonement. The atoning sacrifice of Jesus Christ becomes an effort to reconcile us to God after we have estranged ourselves from Him. From this view, Christ's mission is to repair our damaged relationship with God (rather than to appease the demands of an abstract justice).

We can imagine God as a patient, compassionate Father who, when wronged, does not harbor resentment. Rather, He *initiates* the process of reconciliation. Through His divine Son, He *condescends* to our mortal state (1 Nephi 11:16-33), where He suffers with us when we suffer, mourns with us when we mourn, experiences *everything* we experience:

> And he shall go forth, suffering pains and afflictions and temptations of every kind; and this that the word might be fulfilled which saith he will take upon him the pains and the sicknesses of his people.
>
> And he will take upon him death, that he may loose the bands of death which bind his people; and he will take upon him their infirmities, that his bowels may be filled with mercy, according to the flesh, that he may know according to the flesh how to succor his people according to their infirmities (Alma 7:11-12).

The term used here is "to succor." This word is derived from the Latin term *succurrere*, which means "to run to the rescue of another, or to bring aid." In atoning for us, Christ hurries to our side, selflessly sharing our infirmities so that He might be "filled with compassion" (see, e.g., Mosiah 15:9; 3 Nephi 17:6; D&C

101:9). Indeed, the word *compassion* literally means "to suffer with another." Through it all, He invites us to end our proud and stubborn rebellion and enter into a repaired and renewed relationship with Him.

To live out the Atonement—that is, to become "at one" with God—requires that we respond to this invitation and loving condescension. As the prophet Jacob wrote, "Wherefore, beloved brethren, be reconciled unto him through the atonement of Christ" (Jacob 4:11). When we soften our hearts and accept this invitation to reconcile, Christ helps us become the kinds of beings that enjoy a deep relationship with God. If we have been mistreating our family, reconciling with them involves change. In a similar way, for Christ to reconcile us with God, we must change as people.

We have written a parable to help illustrate this view of the Atonement. Imagine that a son steals several items from his neighbors and his own parents to feed a drug habit. He leaves home, evades the police, and sinks deeper into the destructive lifestyle of the addict. Because of fear, shame, or resentment, he refuses to go home, and ends up in a homeless shelter. In a conventional account of the Atonement, the father could clear the son's record only by serving the son's jail sentence for him and paying the son's debts to the neighbors. However, this would not address the son's relationship-damaging habits and stubborn, prideful heart.

Imagine the father showed up at the homeless shelter with a sleeping bag and, to his son's great surprise, said, "Hi there, Tommy. I've missed you so much. I can't bear for you to be away and suffering like this anymore, so I'm moving in with you." The son may protest and feel remorse that he has brought his father to dwell in such a humble setting. Nonetheless, the father insists that , from now on, he will share evening meals with him, sleep in an adjacent cot, and just *be* with him until he is ready to come back home, where the rest of the family prayerfully awaits.

Of course, the boy must change his priorities and habits before he can truly restore his relationship with his family. The father cannot *make* his son's changes for him. But he can remove every obstacle and excuse, and lovingly walk with him through the process. This loving condescension and grace initiates reconciliation and change, and breaks down whatever walls of pride and resentment the son has placed between him and his parents. Without the father reaching out and humiliating himself with his son, those walls of pride and resentment could grow until they became impenetrable.

In this view, the Atonement plays out less like a cosmic court hearing, and much more like an ongoing, earnest conversation between two friends or family members. God is whole-heartedly inviting mankind to change their ways so that broken relationships can be mended and damaged souls made whole. In a signal of sincerity, our reconciling God has subjected Himself to immeasurable suffering on behalf of His troubled children, to awaken within us a hope for reunion and desire for reconciliation, without which, we would be lost. In this way, the atoning work of Jesus Christ is an ongoing process rather than a single (historical) event, and it involves the Savior coming to us (the condescension of God) at least as much as us coming to Him.

In part because of the penal-substitution theory and other such legalistic theories of the atonement, it can be easy to think of repentance as being about punishment (or avoiding punishment). However, the *person* view of truth offer a different perspective. As Elder Theodore M. Burton has taught:

> The Old Testament was originally written in Hebrew, and the word used in it to refer to the concept of repentance

is *shube*. We can better understand what *shube* means by reading a passage from Ezekiel and inserting the word *shube*, along with its English translation. To the "watchmen" appointed to warn Israel, the Lord says:

"When I say unto the wicked, O wicked man, thou shalt surely die; if thou dost not speak to warn the wicked from his way, that wicked man shall die in his iniquity; but his blood will I require at thine hand. Nevertheless, if thou warn the wicked of his way to turn from [*shube*] it; if he do not turn from [*shube*] his way, he shall die in his iniquity; but thou hast delivered thy soul. ... Say unto them, As I live, saith the Lord God, I have no pleasure in the death of the wicked; but that the wicked turn from [*shube*] his way and live." (Ezek. 33:8–11)

I know of no kinder, sweeter passage in the Old Testament than those beautiful lines. In reading them, can you think of a kind, wise, gentle, loving Father in Heaven pleading with you to *shube*, or turn back to him—to leave unhappiness, sorrow, regret, and despair behind and turn back to your Father's family, where you can find happiness, joy, and acceptance among his other children?

That is the message of the Old Testament. Prophet after prophet writes of *shube*—that turning back to the Lord, where we can be received with joy and rejoicing. The Old Testament teaches time and again that we must turn from evil and do instead that which is noble and good. This means that we must not only change our ways, we must change our very thoughts, which control our actions.[105]

Seen in this way, repentance is a process of turning away from one thing and towards another. It involves leaving aside one way living and stepping into a new way of being—and doing so at the patient, persistent, loving invitation of a Heavenly Father who seeks only the eternal happiness of His children. When we turn away from sin, we cease betraying our covenants and reconcile ourselves with God.

Reframing Our Questions: Chapter 11

Idea-truth: Why did eternal law require Christ to die in order for us to be forgiven?

Person-truth: How does the Atonement help restore our relationship with God?

The first question presumes that Christ's suffering and death bring salvation by appeasing the demands of eternal laws beyond God Himself. Because this presumes more than we actually know, we can get bogged down in questions that we don't have ready answers to. The second question treats Christ's suffering and death as part of God's effort to reconcile with His children, to restore our relationship with Him. Our focus is less on our relationship with abstract moral laws and more on our relationship with God.

Idea-truth: How can I better understand and implement the Atonement in my daily life?

Person-truth: How can I more fully submit to Christ's will and accept His invitation to be "at one" with him and our Heavenly Father?

When we treat the suffering and death of Christ as something we can "apply" to our life, we are treating it as an abstraction.

Picture, for example, the question: "My spouse has suffered deeply and patiently to restore our marriage and rescue me from my bad habits. How can I apply his or her suffering to my daily life?" Put in this way, the question is off-putting, and ends up treating the person as a tool, a means to an end. When we talk about the Atonement of Jesus Christ this way, we borrow the same language we use when we talk about applying abstract principles to particular situations (e.g., *idea*-truth). From a *person*-truth perspective, we might instead use the same language we would use when talking about the reconciling efforts of a friend or family member (for example, "How can I respond to my spouse's patient suffering and set aside the habits, attitudes, worldviews that have alienated us?").

CHAPTER 12

Person-truth in a world of science and reason

The *idea* view of truth serves as the foundation for most modern scientific and scholarly discourse. Latter-day Saints are invested in the idea that good science and good religion can complement each other in perfect harmony and that we can be good disciples and scholars at the same time. This leads to some apparent surface-level contradictions between the central claims of this book and actual practice among Latter-day Saints in scientific and academic discourse. Let's explore this more deeply.

Scientific naturalism suggests that all events in the universe can be accounted for in terms of matter as governed by universal mathematical and scientific laws. Naturalists use reason and observation to discover underlying patterns in the operations of nature. This can be illustrated in the history and development of scientific discourse. Galileo Galilei (1564-1642 AD), for example, believed that nature is "inexorable [and acts only] through immutable laws which she never transgresses."[106]

Robert Boyle (1627-1691 AD) likewise stated: "I look upon

the metaphysical and mathematical principles … to be truths of a transcendent kind that do not properly belong either to philosophy or theology; but are universal foundations and instruments of all the knowledge we mortals can acquire."[107] Boyle even went so far as to speculate that these mathematical principles may be "ultimate truths superior to God himself."[108]

Today, two basic assumptions guide scientists' understanding of the laws of nature: *position symmetry* and *time symmetry*. This means that "the laws of nature are the same everywhere in the universe" and that they "have remained the same through time. They are the same now as they were in the distant past, and they will be the same in the future."[109] In any case, scientific naturalism assumes that what is *ultimately* true can be captured in abstract ideas that are universal, unchangeable, and without context.

Person-truth and science do not conflict

Does this mean that the person view of truth rejects science? Not in the slightest. Many faithful Latter-day Saints have devoted their lives to precisely this kind of scholarship and inquiry, including prophets and apostles. Elder James E. Talmage and Elder John A. Widstoe, for example, were well known for their love of the natural sciences (and were thoroughly naturalistic in their worldview). Prior to his full-time Church service, Elder Richard G. Scott was a nuclear engineer who helped design the first nuclear submarine for the U.S. Navy.

Other famous Latter-day Saints were renowned scientists as well. Melvin Cook and Henry Erying (the father of President Henry B. Erying) were both devoted Latter-day Saints and award-winning chemists. Harvey Fletcher, also a devoted Latter-day Saint, was a physicist known for his work in acoustics and inventor of the first electronic hearing aid. This list could go on indefinitely. Today, there are thousands of Latter-day Saint scholars in the natural sciences who are devoted to their faith while also making rigorous, thoughtful contributions in their disciplines.

Some readers may be suspicious of the distinction between *idea*-truth and *person*-truth because it seems to add fuel to the tiresome conflict between science and religion. We do not think it needs to. We admire those who reconcile a life of scientific inquiry with a life of devoted discipleship. The solution lies in *epistemic humility*. The word *epistemic* refers to knowledge, or how we know things. Epistemic humility simply means that we treat naturalism as a pragmatically useful assumption, rather than as absolute truth.

For example, scientific laws simply describe patterns we observe in the natural world. For example, we observe that things tend to fall in very predictable ways. Falling objects are so predictable, in fact, that we can describe their motion in terms of mathematics, such as the law of gravity. If we know the mass of the planet, and the mass of a second object (whether it be the moon or a shoe), we can predict precisely how the second object is going to fall (or orbit). This is all a perfectly empirical exercise, which means it is based on observed facts of the universe.

But then we often go one step further and treat the law of gravity as an *explanation* rather than as a description. We treat it as if it were a real "thing" out there that can *make* stuff happen. When we do this, we move beyond what empirical evidence can justify. Even though we observe regularities in nature, nothing requires us to believe those patterns are universal or immutable—or that they *cause* our experiences. When we make sweeping metaphysical claims about the world, we leave the realm of science and enter the realm of philosophical speculation.

Here's the point: nothing about science (thought of narrowly as a commitment to empirical evidence) requires us to rigidly adopt an *idea* view of truth. We can provisionally adopt some assumptions of Greek thought when they are useful, *without* adopting them as an inflexible philosophical worldview. There are no frictionless surfaces, perfectly elastic collisions, or free-falling bodies, but these assumptions are useful when making predictions about the world.

From a *person* view of truth, rigorous scholarship can be carried out in conjunction with prayer, covenant making and keeping, and temple worship—with few (if any) intellectual inconsistencies. From this view, the goals of *all* these forms of inquiry are the same: to more fully know God and the workmanship of His hands and to serve our fellow man. President Brigham Young once taught:

> How gladly would we understand every principle pertaining to science and art, and become thoroughly acquainted with every intricate operation of nature, and with all the chemical changes that are constantly going on around us! How delightful this would be, and what a boundless field of truth and power is open for us to explore![110]

President John Taylor also taught:

> Science reveals the beauty and harmony of the world material; it unveils to us ten thousand mysteries in the kingdom of nature, and shows that all forms of life through fire and analogous decay are returned again to its bosom. It unfolds to us the mysteries of cloud and rains, dew and frost, growth and decay, and reveals the operation of those silent irresistible forces which give vitality to the world. It

reveals to us the more wonderful operations of distant orbs and their relations to the forces of nature.[111]

Given our belief in a Divine Creator who is a God of order, it is not at all surprising to us that we find patterns and consistencies in the natural world, or even in human activity and experience. Such patterns are authored by the Truth made Flesh, and bear the mark of His creative work. Science is a systematic method of revealing these useful patterns. But notice the crucial difference here: at no point have we described these patterns as unchangeable, universal, or absolute. We do not have to embrace the *metaphysics* in order to embrace the empirical methods of systematic observation and rational analysis.

This approach also treats science as a *human* enterprise. Its practices and norms are invented by humans, and social forces invariably play into the way researchers do their work.[112] As the Latter-day Saint psychologist and scholar Duane Boyce states: "Recognizing such factors, ... we can be saved from ... dogmatism and instead attain something approaching wisdom: a lingering tentativeness and humility about many of the beliefs we hold at any one time."[113] From the *person* view of truth, we treat scientific conclusions as provisional.

The relationship between reason and truth

In modern thought, for a rational argument to be convincing, it must lay out a series of conclusions that are logically *necessitated* by demonstrable premises. From this view, reason leads us to what *must* be the case, given our premises and the evidence at hand. We can see the Greek roots of this perspective: the conclusions of valid reasoning cannot be different, if the premises are true.

However, from a *person* view of truth, we might see reason as kind of language. As a language, we can use reason to articulate a wide variety of worldviews and perspectives. In this view, reason does not lead to certain conclusions. Two completely rational people can arrive at very different conclusions, depending on their prior beliefs and predispositions.[114] We do not have to pit faith *against* reason. Rather, there are simply more and less faithful ways of making sense of our experiences, and more and less rational ways of making sense of faith.

Richard Williams has proposed that we use two dimensions to talk about the relationship between faith and reason:

> In place of the common conceptual dimension anchored by faith at one end and reason at the other, I suggest that there are really two dimensions. It might be helpful to picture them as perpendicular to one another. One dimension is anchored on one end by reason and on the other end by its opposite: irrationality, promiscuous subjectivity, or even solipsism. The other dimension is anchored on one end by faith and on the other by the opposite of faith.[115]

In keeping with earlier chapters, we think it makes sense to say that the opposite of faith is "infidelity" or "unfaithfulness." In Williams's framework, reason represents different degrees of coherence or persuasiveness in a person's worldview, whereas faith represents different degrees of fidelity (or faithfulness) in our relationship with God.

There are four key quadrants that illustrate ways that faith and reason might play out in actual people's lives (see the figure on the next page). In Quadrant I, there are those who are true to their covenants with God, but who are not good at articulating their worldview in a coherent way to others. In Quadrant IV, there are those who are very coherent, but who are not true to their

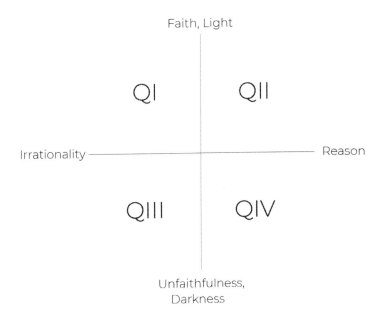

commitments to God or ignore His influence in their lives. They may persuasively lead others away from God. In Quadrant III, there are those live "without God in the world," and who are *also* incoherent, unable to rationally articulate their views. And finally, in Quadrant II, there are those who are faithful to their commitments with God, and who can coherently and persuasively talk to others about their beliefs.

From this view, reason might not lead to a single endpoint but rather to a variety of possibilities on the right side of the chart. Reason can help us better understand God's instructions and persuasively communicate them with others. But when uninformed by the Holy Spirit (or light of Christ), reason can just as easily lead us away from Him. A darkened mind can be as rational as a mind enlightened by the Holy Spirit. Reason can be used to advance God's interests *or* to hedge them up. In short, reason does not assure us access to truth. We must rely on the truth Himself to direct us as we reason together (Isaiah 1:18) in the light of faith. But reason *can* help us make our views more persuasive and coherent.

Reframing Our Questions: Chapter 12

Idea-truth: How can empirical science and rational thought guide us in discovering the workings of the unchanging laws and natural order of the cosmos?

Person-truth: How can we best understand the consistent and reliable patterns we find in nature so as to use that understanding in pragmatic ways to better mankind and serve God?

The first question adopts pre-empirical assumptions about the world (e.g., that the patterns we observe are universal, immutable, impersonal, etc.). These assumptions are not themselves empirically testable, and are thus not an essential part of the scientific enterprise. The second question treats patterns in nature as givens that can be made useful in our pragmatic endeavors in life, without making metaphysical assumptions that are unwarranted by the evidence. *Person*-truth welcomes the idea of searching for patterns and finding meaning in those patterns—we only relinquish the assumption that they must be immutable or universal.

Idea-truth: Which should we trust more: reason or revelation?

Person-truth: How can we use the divine gift of reason to articulate and defend our loyalties to God?

The first question assumes that when we arrive at rational conclusions that differ from divine teaching, we face a conflict that must be resolved. However, instead of seeing reason and revelation as competing paths to truth, we can see them as orthogonal dimensions. From a *person*-truth perspective, we might recognize that ideas that draw us away from Truth (God) can be rendered rational through the artifices of reason. This does not make reason our enemy—ideas that draw us closer to God can *also* be rendered rational through the same means. Reason ceases to be a threat altogether and becomes a tool.

Conclusion

One day, while teaching in the city of Capernaum, Jesus challenged the trust of his followers. He taught them that the Father had sent spiritual bread—manna—from heaven to nourish the children of Israel. Those listening assumed that He was talking about divine teachings that would nourish their hearts and minds. They said, "Lord, evermore give us this bread" (John 6:34).

To this question, Jesus replied, "I am the bread of life: he that cometh to me shall never hunger; and he that believeth on me shall never thirst. ... I am the bread which came down from heaven" (John 6:35, 41). In other words, Christ was not there to *give* them nourishing words from God—He *was* the bread that would nourish them. Despite their Hebrew heritage, many of those who listened did not like this response. We read,

> From that *time* many of his disciples went back, and walked no more with him.
>
> Then said Jesus unto the twelve, Will ye also go away?
>
> Then Simon Peter answered him, Lord, to whom shall

we go? thou hast the words of eternal life.

And we believe and are sure that thou art that Christ, the Son of the living God (John 6:66-69).

Peter's response is important: "Lord, to *whom* shall we go?" They were sure that Jesus was the Son of God. Even if they did not fully understand what He taught—only later would John describe Jesus as the Word, rather than merely *having* words—they knew no one else who claimed the same divine commission. The question at hand was not, "*What* should we believe?" but rather, "*Who* has divine authority?"

Many of the beliefs and practices of the Latter-day Saint community simply do not make sense in the modern world. To use an analogy, encountering Hebrew thought today might be as bewildering as encountering the lion Aslan on the bridge of the starship *Enterprise*. The universe of C. S. Lewis's Narnia is fundamentally different from the universe of *Star Trek*—the moral assumptions that saturate the *Chronicles of Narnia* would appear foreign to characters such as Spock, Captain Kirk, or Doctor McCoy.

Similarly, Hebrew thought may appear irrational from the perspective of Greek philosophy, and the *person* view of truth may look bizarre to those acculturated into an *idea* view of truth. This is why many of the questions we ask—however simple and honest they may seem—simply do not have immediate answers. It is because our questions implicitly assume a Greek world, and we are dealing with a Hebrew faith. The *idea* view of truth (and its Greek assumptions) has made Hebrew tradition and belief look like *nonsense*.

However, these same beliefs and practices make perfect sense if we see the world with Hebrew eyes and adopt a *person* view of truth. When we know the differences between Greek and Hebrew thought, we can develop a richer understanding of our beliefs.

Matthew Arnold, a British poet, once incisively wrote, "Hebraism and Hellenism [another term for Greek philosophy]—between these two points of influence moves our world."[116] When we tease out the influences of each, we can better frame questions about our faith.

We will use polygamy as our case example. When we adopt a Greek view, we might ask the question, "How can we reconcile Joseph Smith's practice of polygamy with the Book of Mormon's condemnation of polygamy?" This question assumes that there is a broad principle—a universal moral code—that makes rational sense of God's varying instructions. But from a Hebrew perspective, we might ask instead, "What does God requires of us in the here and now? Are the apostles and prophets who lead us today commissioned by Him?"

When we adopt an *idea* view of truth, we might ask God, "Is the doctrine of polygamy a true (or false) doctrine?" Our concern is whether certain ideas are "truth." When we ask these sorts of questions, we may or may not receive the answers we seek. But when we adopt a *person* view of truth, we might ask God, "How can I be a better spouse? How can I invite your hand into my marriage? What can I do to serve you in my family responsibilities?" Our concern *here* is our relationship with God and others—how we can fulfill our covenants duties to God and our family.

Consider the sorts of questions that God answered in the scriptures. When Nephi was instructed to build a ship, he asked, "Lord, whither shall I go that I may find ore to molten, that I may make tools to construct the ship after the manner which thou hast shown unto me?" (1 Nephi 17:9). Nephi's question was one of action, not doctrine—how he could serve God and fulfill His commandments. When Aaron taught the Lamanite King about the plan of salvation, the king asked:

What shall I do that I may have this eternal life of which thou hast spoken? Yea, what shall I do that I may be born of God, having this wicked spirit rooted out of my breast, and receive his Spirit, that I may be filled with joy, that I may not be cast off at the last day? (Alma 22:15).

Shortly after, the king prayed and asked God, "O God, Aaron hath told me that there is a God; and if there is a God, and if thou art God, wilt thou make thyself known unto me, and I will give away all my sins to know thee" (Alma 22:18). These sorts of questions presume a *person*-truth—and these are the sorts of questions that find answers.

When this happens, our testimony becomes a testimony of Christ and His redeeming grace in our hearts and minds, not a testimony of abstract doctrines. The Church and its institutions become less a system of abstract belief than tools that help us make covenants and live out our moral duties. We begin to see God's influence in our communities as we fulfill our callings and responsibilities. And we become sure—with a surety grounded in personal experience—that the Church was established by God and is lead by Him, even if it is administered by mortal people. And we become sure of God's hand in our own life, and He unfolds His purposes to us.

Before we close this book, we want to caution our readers. We do not claim that the Hebrews had everything right. After all, the Old and New Testaments are full of stories about Hebrews getting things *wrong*. Recall Nephi's warning against adopting all the ways of the Jews of his time, "for their works were works of darkness, and their doings were doings of abominations" (2 Nephi 25:2). It would be a mistake to assume that *everything* about the Greek worldview is corrupt while *everything* about the Hebrew worldview is pure.

In addition, we treat the ideas in this book as a useful *heuristic*, that is, a broad-brush-stroke mental "rule of thumb" or "guideline." If we take the ideas in this book too rigidly, we are bound to end up in trouble. This book is itself a conceptual framework, a *set of ideas*. It should be treated like every other ideological perspective: useful whenever it strengthens our covenant relationship with God, dangerous when it alienates us from God. For example, nothing in this book should be used to rationalize moral relativism or. There *are* reliable patterns in human experience, and most of God's commandments will *not* change willy-nilly from decade to decade. Our hope is simply to avoid *both* the extremes of moral relativism and dogmatic absolutism.

And, most importantly, we will be less likely to mistake abstract philosophical systems for the divine, embodied Truth we worship. We do not reject philosophy or abstract ideas altogether. This book is, after all, written in the *Greek* tradition. If we were writing in the Hebrew tradition, we might have simply told stories instead—stories about people's experiences with God. We agree with Slife and Reber, who wrote:

> We do not advocate the rejection of [abstract ideas] altogether. We need theories to help organize and make sense of things and events. However, we do not have to make our theories into truths. ... The problem is that such principles can ultimately hamper our recognition of the truth that is there (concretely) in the ... room with us—the Holy Spirit.[117]

This applies for the abstract ideas discussed in *this* book. Do not adopt these ideas in inflexible ways that might lead you to ignore correction from the Truth Himself or from His chosen servants. We have failed if our readers adopt our approach as a dogmatic theology of its own. We will be deeply troubled if readers use our ideas disparage or criticize prophets and apostles who teach and warn the Church. Not every leader of the Church will agree with our perspective. This in no way diminishes their stewardship as the Lord's appointed servants. If we take our approach seriously, the words of the living Christ as delivered by His chosen servants in the here-and-now take precedence over the reasoning of men, no matter how nuanced such reasoning might be.

Our final caveat is, perhaps, the most important. We believe that our view can help us navigate the intellectual and spiritual labyrinths of our day. That said, we do not have to know anything about philosophy to live a life of faithful, dedicated discipleship. To borrow a phrase from James Faulconer, "the proverbial farmer in Santaquin" can live a devoted life without ever learning about philosophy or the history of ideas.[118] We genuinely hope this book is illuminating for our readers, but we certainly do not believe that understanding any of it is *essential* to keeping our covenants with God (even if, at times, it may be *useful*).

If you are unconvinced by our perspective, but you keep your covenants with God and faithfully serve in the Church, that is great! If we take our own perspective seriously, then we *shouldn't* be too worried if others don't see things quite like we do, as long as they live out their covenants with God. If the viewpoint in this book strengthens your commitment to God and your willingness to serve in His kingdom, then that is *also* great. Our main goal is to help readers focus on their relationship with Christ and value their participation in the Church.

Our goal has been to explore some of the implications of our Israelite heritage. As we stated in the introduction, we echo the words of Nephi, who wrote, "For the fulness of mine intent is that I may persuade men to come unto the God of Abraham, and the

God of Isaac, and the God of Jacob, and be saved" (1 Nephi 6:4). We want our readers to come to know God through prayer, by studying His words, by living His commandments, by participating in the rituals and ceremonies of His holy temple, and by heeding the words of His modern-day prophets and apostles. These things will help us to come to *know* God, rather than merely knowing about Him. Our goal is to witness the hand of God in our lives so that we can testify of our *own* experiences with the Almighty.

Further Readings

Further readings about Truth as a Person

Brent D. Slife, "C.S. Lewis: Drawn by the Truth Made Flesh," in Andrew C. Skinner and Robert L. Millet, eds., *C.S. Lewis, the Man and His Message: An LDS Perspective* (Salt Lake City: Bookcraft, 1990), 20-37.

Brent Slife and Jeff Reber, "Comparing the Practical Implications of Secular and Christian Truth in Psychotherapy," in Aaron P. Jackson, Lane Fischer, and Doris R. Dant, eds., *Turning Freud Upside Down* (Provo: BYU Press, 2005), 160-182.

James Faulconer, "Truth, Virtue, and Perspectivism," in *Virtue and the Abundant Life* (Salt Lake City, UT: Deseret Book, 2012), 80.

Richard N. Williams, "Faithful Knowing and Virtuous Acts," in *Virtue and the Abundant Life* (Salt Lake City, Utah: Deseret Book, 2012), 62.

Further readings about Greek and Hebrew thought

James Faulconer, "Appendix 2: Hebrew versus Greek Thinking," in *Scripture Study: Tools and Suggestions* (Provo, UT: BYU Press,

FARMS, 1999), 135-153.

Marvin R. Wilson, *Our Father Abraham: The Jewish Roots of the Christian Faith* (Grand Rapids, MI: William B. Eerdmans Publishing Company, 1989).

Marvin R. Wilson, *Exploring Our Hebraic Heritage: A Christian Theology of Roots and Renewal* (Grand Rapids, MI: William B. Eerdmans Publishing Company, 2014).

Thorleif Boman, *Hebrew Thought Compared with Greek*, trans. Jules L. Moreau (New York, NY: Norton, 1960).

Norman H. Snaith, *The Distinctive Ideas of the Old Testament* (New York, NY: Schocken Books, 1964), 159.

Thomas Cahill, *Sailing the Wine-Dark Sea: Why the Greeks Matter* (New York, NY: Doubleday, 2003), 259.

Thomas Cahill, *The Gift of the Jews: How a Tribe of Desert Nomads Changed the Way Everyone Thinks and Feels* (New York, NY: Doubleday, 1998).

E. Randolph Richards and Brandon J. O'Brien, *Misreading Scripture with Western Eyes: Removing Cultural Blinders to Better Understand the Bible* (Downers Grove, IL: InterVarsity Press, 2012), 182.

Jonathan A. Jacobs (Ed.), *Judaic Sources and Western Thought: Jerusalem's Enduring Presence* (Oxford, UK: Oxford University Press, 2011).

Yoram Hazony, *The Philosophy of Hebrew Scripture* (Cambridge, UK: Cambridge University Press, 2012).

David Patterson, *Hebrew Language and Jewish Thought* (London, UK: RoutledgeCurzon, 2005).

Richard E. Nisbett, *The Geography of Thought: How Asians and Westerners Think Differently ... and Why*. (New York: Free Press, 2003).

Henry Jansen, *Relationality and the Concept of God* (Amsterdam, The Netherlands: Rodopi, 1995).

Murray H. Lichtenstein, "An Interpersonal Theology of the Hebrew Bible" (Alice Ogden Bellis and Joel S. Kaminsky, *Jews, Christians, and the Theology of the Hebrew Scriptures*, Atlanta, GA: Society of Biblical Literature).

George Adam Smith, "The Hebrew Genius as Exhibited in the Old Testament," in Edwyn R. Bevan and Charles Singer, eds., *The Legacy of Israel* (Oxford, UK: Clarendon Press, 1944).

Further readings about the Great Apostasy and Restoration

Noel B. Reynolds, "What Went Wrong for the Early Christians?" In Noel B. Reynolds (Ed.), *Early Christians in Disarray: Contemporary LDS Perspectives on the Christian Apostasy* (Provo, UT: BYU Press, FARMS, 2005).

Noel B. Reynolds, "The Decline of Covenant in Early Christian Thought," in Noel B. Reynolds (Ed.), *Early Christians in Disarray: Contemporary LDS Perspectives on the Christian Apostasy* (Provo, UT: BYU Press, FARMS, 2005).

Daniel W. Graham and James L. Siebach, "The Introduction of Philosophy into Early Christianity," in Noel B. Reynolds (Ed.), *Early Christians in Disarray: Contemporary LDS Perspectives on the Christian Apostasy* (Provo, UT: BYU Press, FARMS, 2005).

John Sanders, "Historical Considerations," in *The Openness of*

God, ed. Clark Pinnock (Downers Grove, IL: InterVarsity Press, 1994).

Dallin H. Oaks, "Apostasy and Restoration," *Ensign*, May 1995, 84-87.

David Thomas, *Hebrew Roots of Mormonism* (Springville, UT: Cedar Fort, 2013).

Richard Hopkins, *How Greek Philosophy Corrupted the Christian Concept of God* (Springville, UT: Horizon Publishers, 2009).

Further readings about science and reason in a world of *Person*-truth

Brent D. Slife and Richard N. Williams, *What's Behind the Research? Discovering Hidden Assumptions in the Behavioral Sciences* (Thousand Oaks, CA: Sage Publications, 1995).

LaMar E. Garrard, "God, Natural Law, and the Doctrine and Covenants," in *Doctrines for Exaltation: Sidney B. Sperry Symposium*, February, 1989 (Salt Lake City, UT: Deseret Book, 1989).

Richard Williams, "Faith, Reason, Knowledge, and Truth," devotional address given at Brigham Young University, February 1, 2000.

Stephen C. Yanchar and Amy Fisher Smith, "Gospel Law and Natural Law," in Aaron P. Jackson, Lane Fischer, and Doris R. Dant, eds., *Turning Freud Upside Down* (Provo: BYU Press, 2005), 10-35.

More on Greek and Hebrew Thought

The central distinction of this book is between the *idea* view of truth and the *person* view of truth. This distinction maps roughly (but not perfectly) onto the central differences between a Greek and Hebrew view of the world. There are other implications of Greek and Hebrew thought that do not map onto the differences between the *idea* view of truth and the *person* view of truth, but which we still wanted to share.

Because Greek thought (broadly understood) prioritizes what does *not* change as more fundamental than what *does* change, Greek thought might lead us to see human nature as fixed and unchangeable. For example, if at certain times you are sad but at other times you are cheery and pleasant, then your *mood* is not part of your essential identity. However, your temperament—that is, the *averages* of your mood swings, and your *general* demeanor—may be more static and more central to your character.

Psychologists often talk about an individual's "personality," which they define as "a pattern of relatively *permanent* traits and unique characteristics that give both *consistency* and individuality to a person's behavior."[119] In other words, personality and identity are those attributes that remain stable across contexts and situations. From this view, to ask someone to change their personality is asking them to do the impossible. Indeed, such a request would be deeply insulting, as it implies that a core part of the person is lacking.

Hebrew thought, on the other hand, might lead us to view our identity as bound up in *activity*. From this perspective, life is about change—changing who we are, changing our relationships with others and God, and through that change fulfilling the purpose of life, which is to see what we and God can make of ourselves. From this perspective, there is nothing particularly unchangeable about our identity. Change is not only a possibility but part of who we are; to live *is* to change, and who we *are* is defined by our *activity* in the world.

For example, as we described earlier, the Hebrew language emphasizes *activity* rather than *stasis* (as Greek and other Indo-European languages do). In the Hebrew language, things are not defined in terms of what is unchanging about them, but by what they *do* and how they operate in a specific context of relations and meanings. James Faulconer explains:

> As latter-day Greeks, we think of the being of persons on analogy with the being of static, inanimate objects. However, in Hebrew thinking, the being of objects is in analogy to the being of living, animate persons. ... We usually think of stasis as originary and movement as a change from that originary state. In Hebrew thinking, however, remaining the same—stasis—is a particular kind of movement. ...
> The Hebrew concept of being means that to be a person

is to do what persons do. The person *is* because he or she is alive, and life—an activity, not a state—is, for Hebrew thought, the essence of what it means to be. Thus the *way* something is defines *what* it is. ... In contrast, Greek thought separates the way of being from the being. In the Greek way of thinking, I am a human being because I have the essence of being human as part of what I am, and how I live my life is irrelevant to whether I am human. In Hebrew thought, however, *how* something is and *what* it is are inseparable.[120]

In other words, in a Hebrew worldview, who we are is defined by our ongoing activities and relationships, not by what is *unchanging* about us. The implications of this simple idea are staggering. If our core identity is not fixed but in *flux,* then we can change *who we are* by changing *what we do* (and how we do it). Through repentance (a change in our behavior and our relationship with God), we can change our very *nature*—with the help of Christ, of course. Alma, after his conversion to Christ, taught:

> Marvel not that all mankind, yea, men and women, all nations, kindreds, tongues and people, must be born again; yea, born of God, changed from their carnal and fallen state, to a state of righteousness, being redeemed of God, becoming his sons and daughters; And thus they become new creatures; and unless they do this, they can in nowise inherit the kingdom of God (Alma 27:25-26).

Just as we should not marvel that we must change (according to Alma), in Hebrew thought, we do not need to marvel that we *can* change. This does not mean it is easy to drop bad habits or to relinquish deeply engrained patterns of thought and behavior. This also does not mean that temptation can be willed away by conscious choice. It simply means that our core being is not etched in stone, and that there is the *possibility* of change, even if change takes time. Greek thought does not allow for this possibility, whereas Hebrew thought does.

This can influence how we think of the final judgment and the purpose of mortality. We learn from Abraham that the Earth was created at least partially as a test for God's children: "And we will prove them herewith, to see if they will do all things whatsoever the Lord their God shall command them" (Abraham 3:25). What this verse means, however, depends quite a bit on whether we see our inner nature as fixed and immutable, or as dynamic and in flux.

If we think of human identity as unchangeable, the test of life is to discover our inner nature and true identity. From this view, the test of life is like a spectrograph—it reveals the essential elements already within us that may have previously been hidden (from ourselves or God).* The purpose of mortality is to put us in situations where our nature is made manifest in behavior (thought, word, and deed). From this perspective, if someone is resurrected into the celestial kingdom, his or her choices were simply manifestations of a latent celestial nature. Ultimately, this Greek-inspired perspective makes the idea of repentance—real, lasting change in the soul—difficult to understand. Our desires, habits, inclinations, and attitudes are seen as a reflection of *who we really are*.

In contrast, if we see human nature as bound up in our actions, we understand the final judgment and the purpose of life quite differently. In this perspective, whether we are "celestial material" or "telestial material" is entirely up for revision *at any time*. As moral agents, it is up to us in each moment whose voice

---

* A spectrograph is a scientific instrument that reflects light off of an unknown substance, such as a mineral. Researchers determine what elements are within the substance by observing the wavelengths of the reflected light.

we will "[list] to obey" (Alma 3:27) and in whose image we will seek to be re-made. This perspective makes the most sense of our culpability for sin, for how can we be judged for being something that we did not *choose* to be?

Seen in this way, life is a test to determine what we will *make* of ourselves (with Christ), not to see which already-existing nature gets revealed. As Elder Dallin H. Oaks teaches: "[T]he Final Judgment is not just an evaluation of a sum total of good and evil acts—what we have *done*. It is an acknowledgment of the final effect of our acts and thoughts—what we have *become*."[121] Elder Oak's language would not make sense if our inner nature is unchangeable and static, since it implies that *who we are* is dynamic and in flux.

We can illustrate the difference between these two views by asking, "What is it that makes us sinners?" A "Greek" way to think about it is that once we have committed a sin, we are by definition *sinners*. And once having done so, there is no way to go back—without divine aid, our being sinners is a static, unchangeable condition. A "Hebrew" way to think about this, however, is that being a *sinner* means having a heart or lifestyle of sin. In this view, by relinquishing our sinful hearts and changing our lifestyles, we can cease to be sinners. It is a malleable condition, rather than a permanent one.

Neither of these views denies the necessity of Christ. The first view treats Christ as necessary because once we have become sinners, only Christ can remove the stain of past sin. The second view treats Christ as necessary because only through Christ's transforming grace can we be remade as people and step into a new and holier way of living, and a renewed relationship with God. We cannot escape the attitudes, habits, and worldviews of sin by ourselves. We need the rescuing activity of Christ and His atonement to free us from the grasp of sin.

Nephi taught that when God's children are resurrected and brought into judgment, "if their works have been filthiness they must needs be filthy; and if they be filthy it must needs be that they cannot dwell in the kingdom of God" (1 Ne. 15:33). If we approach this scripture from a Greek perspective, we might read it this way: "If they have a filthy nature, then the result will be that their works are filthiness." However, when we read the same passage with Hebrew eyes, Nephi is saying that our nature is *determined*, not revealed, by our actions.

In modern thought, family relationships are defined in a *static*, biological sense: a father is a father by virtue of his *genetic* relationship with his children, something that cannot be changed. However, there are different ways of understanding what it means to be a father. As one student of the Hebrew language, Jeff Benner, has suggested: "Even the Hebrew nouns for father and mother are descriptive of action. The Hebrew word for father is אב (av) and literally means 'the one who gives strength to the family' and mother אם (em) means 'the one that binds the family together.'[122]

When seen in this way, to be a father is to do those things that give strength to the family and to be a mother is to do those things that bind the family together. To be a father is to engage in genuine *fathering*. To be a mother is to *mother* one's family. They are both verbs that describe a way of life, a way of relating to another. For this reason, if we draw our strength from Christ, He can quite literally become our father. This changes the way read King Benjamin's teachings:

> And now, because of the covenant which ye have made ye shall be called the children of Christ, his sons, and his daughters; for behold, this day he hath spiritually begotten you; for ye say that your hearts are changed through faith

on his name; therefore, ye are born of him and have become his sons and his daughters (Mosiah 5:7).

From a Hebrew point of view, this reads less like an adoption contract and more like the sensible consequence of heeding Christ's instructions and drawing strength from Him. Also, when we cease to draw strength from Him (by betraying our covenants), He can cease to be our father. In this way, our activities and choices reveal who we are, not because they stem from an inner, immutable nature, but because they determine the kinds of relationships we have with God and others.

The scriptures sometimes use harsh language to describe those who live in sin. King Benjamin, for example, stated: "For the natural man is an enemy to God, and has been from the fall of Adam, and will be, forever and ever" (Mosiah 3:19). When Martin Harris lost 116 pages of the translated manuscript of the Book of Mormon, the Lord told Joseph Smith, "Now, behold, I say unto you, that because you delivered up those writings which you had power given unto you to translate ... into the hands of a wicked man, you have lost them" (D&C 10:1).

To modern sensibilities, this seems harsh: The natural man is an *enemy* to God? Martin Harris, who had no conscious intentions of hindering God's work, a *wicked* man? This seems harsh because we usually describe people in terms of what is *unchanging* about them. But from a Hebrew perspective, wickedness is *always* a (potentially) temporary state of the soul. Someone can be wicked in one moment, and righteous in the next—depending on their activities. King Benjamin, for example, continued:

> For the natural man is an enemy to God, and has been from the fall of Adam, and will be, forever and ever, *unless he yields to the enticings of the Holy Spirit, and putteth off the*

natural man and becometh a saint through the atonement of Christ the Lord" (Mosiah 3:19).

In other words, the natural man is not some unchanging characteristic of the soul but is simply the state of the soul when we are rebelling against the Lord. We can *put off* the natural man—we can *yield* to the invitations of the Holy Spirit. When the scriptures refer to people as wicked, or as sinners, or as enemies of God, no *permanent* identity is attributed to anyone. These are what we call "divine insults," which are insulting only if we adopt Greek assumptions and think they refer to something unchangeable about us.

We ought to love those who make bad choices and consider them *persons* worthy of respect—not because they are *good* people (as if only good people deserve respect and love), but because they are *people*. Further, no matter how good or bad a person is at the moment, there is *always* the possibility of genuine change. President Thomas S. Monson taught, "We have the responsibility to see individuals not as they *are* but rather as they can *become*. I would plead with you to think of them in this way."[123] To do this, we must see ourselves and others through Hebrew eyes, and see that who we *are* is bound up in what we *do*.

Questions and answers

In this chapter, we answer questions that readers may have about the differences between *idea*-truth and *person*-truth.

Isn't God subject to natural law?

Some Latter-day Saint scholars have argued that the personal, relational truth of the scriptures exists within a larger, fundamentally Greeklike universe. From this view, God's power is based on his superior knowledge of abstract, universal scientific laws. For example, Elder Widstoe argued, "God is part of nature, and superior to it only in the sense that the electrician is superior to the current that is transmitted along the wire. The great laws of nature are immutable, and even God cannot transcend them."[124]

Elder Parley P. Pratt suggested the laws that govern the physical world "are absolute and unchangeable in their nature, and apply to all intelligent agencies which do or can exist. They, therefore, apply with equal force to the great, supreme, Eternal Father of the heavens and of the earth, and to His meanest subjects."[125] Elder B. H. Roberts wrote, "Miracles are not, properly speaking, events which take place in violation of the laws of nature, but … they take place through the operation of higher laws of nature not yet understood by man."[126]

This popular perspective seems to reconcile the person view of truth with the idea view of truth. However, this approach requires us to adopt the idea view of truth, and its Greek assumptions about the world. It subjugates the Hebrew worldview of scripture into a fundamentally Greek conceptual framework. As Garrard points out, "In such a universe it would be more reasonable for people to worship the law (which incidentally has no body, parts, or passions) since it is more powerful than God and he is subject to it."[127]

When we do this, we run the risk of creating a Hellenized version of a fundamentally Hebrew faith (which is what early Christian scholars did). In fact, this view adopts the same Greek philosophical ideas as Hellenized Christianity. Although it changes the conceptual category God occupies, it does not challenge any of its underlying assumptions about truth (see the figure on the next page). It embraces the Greek assumption that fundamental reality *must* be abstract and incorporeal.

We do *not* claim that those who hold this view are apostate or are leading the Church into apostasy. The inspired teachings of Elder Pratt, Elder Widstoe, and Elder Talmage can be taken in a different light. Their ultimate goal was to convince Latter-day Saints that they can pursue scientific endeavors and not relinquish their faith. As Brigham Young taught, "Our religion will not clash with or contradict the facts of science in any particular."[128] This is a vital message that has been repeated by nearly every prophet since.

In addition, prophets and apostles have been inconsistent on

Greek Thought

unchangeable without context non-physical	{	forms essences mathematical truths universal laws	things people facts cultures	}	changing contextual physical

Hellenized Christianity

unchangeable without context non-physical	{	God	things people facts cultures	}	changing contextual physical

Hellenized Mormonism

unchangeable without context non-physical	{	forms essences mathematical truths universal laws	things people facts cultures God	}	changing contextual physical

this issue. For evidence, we read that God "hath given a law unto all things, by which they move in their times and their seasons; and their courses are fixed, even the courses of the heavens and the earth, which comprehend the earth and all the planets" (D&C 88:42-43). This implies that God *decreed* natural law. Similarly, President Brigham Young taught:

> It is hard to get the people to believe that God is a scientific character, that He lives by science or strict law, that by this He is, and by law he was made what He is; and will remain to all eternity because of His faithful adherence to law. It is a most difficult thing to make the people believe that every art and science and all wisdom comes from Him, and that He is their Author.[129]

At first glance, it seems that Brother Brigham agrees with Elders Pratt, Widstoe, and Roberts. But he is actually saying something very different. Brigham Young describes God as a "scientific character," but then claims that God is the *Author* of scientific law. However, the scientific laws of Greek thought do not have authors. They are immutable, embedded in the fabric of the universe.

On another occasion, President Young taught: "Our religion embraces chemistry; it embraces all the knowledge of the geologist, and then it goes a little further than their systems of argument, for the Lord almighty, its author, is the greatest chemist there is."[130] But notice that God is *not* a chemist in the same way that *we* can be chemists (in mortality, at least), because chemists do not *author* the laws of chemistry. Brigham Young is teaching that God is familiar with and often works through scientific laws, but also implies (with imprecise language, perhaps) that such laws are *decreed.* The prophet Joseph Smith taught:

> God has made certain decrees which are fixed and immovable; for instance, God set the sun, the moon, and the stars in the heavens, and *gave them their laws,* conditions and bounds, which they cannot pass *except by His commandments;* they all move in perfect harmony i n their sphere and order, and are as lights, wonders and signs unto us.[131]

When Joseph Smith describes these laws as "fixed and immovable," he is certainly not using these terms in the Greek sense. He implies that heavenly bodies *could* defy these laws when commanded by God. They are fixed and immovable only to *us.* Joseph Smith taught, "If the veil were rent today, and the great God *who holds this world in its orbit,* and who upholds all worlds and all things by his power, was to make himself visible ... you would see him like a man in form—like yourselves."[132] In the Book of Mormon, we read:

> For behold, the dust of the earth moveth hither and thither, to the dividing asunder, at the command of our great and everlasting God.
>
> Yea, behold at his voice do the hills and the mountains tremble and quake.
>
> And by the power of his voice they are broken up, and become smooth, yea, even like unto a valley.
>
> Yea, by the power of his voice doth the whole earth shake; Yea, by the power of his voice, do the foundations rock, even to the very center.
>
> Yea, and if he say unto the earth—Move—it is moved.
>
> Yea, if he say unto the earth—Thou shalt go back, that it lengthen out the day for many hours—it is done;
>
> And thus, according to his word the earth goeth back, and it appeareth unto man that the sun standeth still; yea, and behold, this is so; for surely it is the earth that moveth and not the sun (Helaman 12:8-15).

In conclusion, we can make a strong case that the physical universe *does* operate within a system of observable law that is detectable by empirical observation, but also that these laws ultimately answer to God (who can override them).

What of Justice and Mercy in the Book of Mormon?

We often read these passages wrong, because we read them with Greek eyes. We import *idea*-truth assumptions into the text. Here is the passage in question (written by Alma to his son Corianton):

And thus we see that all mankind were fallen, and they were in the grasp of justice; yea, the justice of God, which consigned them forever to be cut off from his presence.

And now, the plan of mercy could not be brought about except an atonement should be made; therefore God himself atoneth for the sins of the world, to bring about the plan of mercy, to appease the demands of justice, that God might be a perfect, just God, and a merciful God also. ...

But there is a law given, and a punishment affixed, and a repentance granted; which repentance, mercy claimeth; otherwise, justice claimeth the creature and executeth the law, and the law inflicteth the punishment; if not so, the works of justice would be destroyed, and God would cease to be God (Alma 42:14-15, 22).

It is easy to interpret these verses as talking about Justice and Mercy as abstract laws that God Himself is beholden to (or "God would cease to be God"). When we take a person view of truth seriously, though, we can reread these scriptures. Alma uses the terms *justice* and *mercy* to depict two different states of the soul, or ways of being in relation with God. *Justice* refers to our separation or alienation from God: "And thus we see that all mankind were fallen, and they were in the grasp of justice; yea, the justice of God, which consigned them forever to be cut off from his presence" (Alma 42:14). *Mercy* refers to reconciliation with God.

Simply put, if sin is rebellion against God, we cannot be reconciled with God while sinning. Can we "rebel" against someone, *and* not be at odds with them (i.e., reconciled)? If we could be reunited with God while still living in the midst of sin, there would be no *justice* (that is, separation from God due to sin) in the first place. The concept itself would be meaningless. Alma describes this as "mercy destroying justice." If sin really does alienate us from God, then mercy—that is, reunion and reconciliation with God—can *only* happen on conditions of repentance (that is, the cessation of sin and rebellion).

And that's why we need Christ. Through the Atonement, Christ empowers us to change our ways, lay aside our sinful habits and lifestyles, and become new creatures in Christ. Without this, Alma teaches, "there was no means to reclaim men from this fallen state, which man had brought upon himself because of his own disobedience" (Alma 42:12). In this way, the Atonement brings about mercy (that is, reconciliation with God) while at the same time preserving justice (that is, alienation from God due to sin), by helping us return to God as changed people. Amulek taught the Zoramites:

> And thus [Christ] shall bring salvation to all those who shall believe on his name; this being the intent of this last sacrifice, to bring about the bowels of mercy, which overpowereth justice, and bringeth about means unto men that they may have faith unto repentance.
>
> And thus mercy can satisfy the demands of justice, and encircles them in the arms of safety, while he that exercises no faith unto repentance is exposed to the whole law of the demands of justice; therefore only unto him that has faith unto repentance is brought about the great and eternal plan of redemption (Alma 34:15-16).

It might be fruitful to read these verses in this way: "This is the intent of this last sacrifice, to initiate a reconciliation of man with God, which overpowereth the separation caused by sin and rebellion, *because* it bringeth about means unto men that they may have faith to change their lives and lay down their instruments of rebellion, and thereby restore their relationship with God." Christ's sacrifice does not so much appease the demands of cosmic law as it invites us to change our ways and reconcile with God. In this way, it overpowers our separation from God due to sin, without undoing the very concept of sin and separation in the first place.

Why would God cease to be God, if sin did not separate us from Him? James Faulconer explains that in Hebrew thought, *identity* is bound up in *activity*. Things (or persons) *are* what they *do*. If something (or someone) changes what it *does*, it changes what it *is*, as well the relations it has with others. "Though God has a particular form," he writes, "for Hebrew, to be God is not necessarily to have that particular form. To be God is not to fit under a particular logical, biological, or ontological category but to live and act in a particular way, namely, the godly way."[133]

So when Alma tells us that God would cease to be God if He were to cease holding us morally accountable for rebellion and pride, he may just be telling us something about what it means to be a God. Justice and mercy are ways in which our Heavenly Father *acts* as God rather than Greeklike abstract laws independent of Him. He holds us accountable for our actions and yet reconciles us with Him when we are willing. As Elder D. Todd Christofferson explains, "A God who makes no demands is the functional equivalent of a God who does not exist."[134]

If rebellion, pride, and enmity no longer alienated us from God, this would profoundly alter what it means for Him to be our God. He would no longer be the God of Abraham, Isaac, and Jacob.

Doesn't the Book of Mormon describe God as unchangeable?

The ancient prophet Moroni wrote:

> Do we not read that God is the same yesterday, today, and forever, and in him there is no variableness neither shadow of changing?
>
> And now, if ye have imagined up unto yourselves a god who doth vary, and in whom there is shadow of changing, then have ye imagined up unto yourselves a god who is not a God of miracles (Mormon 9:9-10).

And, somewhat further on, Moroni asks:

> And who shall say that Jesus Christ did not do many mighty miracles? And there were many mighty miracles wrought by the hands of the apostles.
>
> And if there were miracles wrought then, why has God ceased to be a God of miracles and yet be an unchangeable Being? And behold, I say unto you he changeth not; if so he would cease to be God; and he ceaseth not to be God, and is a God of miracles (Mormon 9:18-19).

From a Greek perspective, these passages seem to clearly refer to a universal truth and the immutable nature of God. If we read the verses from this perspective, then we might conclude that if God's servants deliver differing or conflicting instructions in two comparable contexts (which cannot be easily reduced to an abstract, universal principle), then one of those instructions is likely wrong.

However, these passages can be easily interpreted differently. In context, Moroni reiterates the fact that God is *active* in the world. He communicates with His children, performs miracles, bestows spiritual gifts, and so forth. We can interpret Moroni as arguing that a God who is not active in the world is a God who does not exist at all. To deny the revelations of God, to deny the existence of spiritual gifts and miracles is to deny the very *existence* of God as a living, personal, and relational being in the world. An inactive, theoretical God, whose hand is not manifest in our lives and communities, is not the living God of Israel.

The above passages (and others like them—see, e.g., Moroni 8:18, D&C 20:17, and D&C 104:2—assure us that God is a thoroughly reliable, covenant-making and promise-keeping being. Jaroslav Pelikan, one of the most famous scholars of Christian history, has written:

> In Judaism it was possible simultaneously to ascribe change of purpose to God and to declare that God did not change, without resolving the paradox; for the immutability of God was seen as the trustworthiness of his covenanted relation to his people in the concrete history of his judgment and mercy, rather than as a primarily ontological category. [135]

God's instructions *do* change from time to time, depending on the circumstances and choices of His children. But He is nonetheless utterly and completely reliable in His promises, and unfailing in His redemptive activity toward those who serve Him. In other words, God does not betray His commitments to His children, and He does indeed have patterns that He frequently follows. He is neither fickle nor arbitrary. And He can be described this way without attributing some sort of *metaphysical* unchangeability to Him. What makes the God of the Restoration the God of the Old and New Testament is not that His instructions are identical, but that it is the same heavenly being who gives them.

Don't the scriptures describe God's commandments as "irrevocable"?

In the Doctrine and Covenants we read, "There is a law, irrevocably decreed in heaven before the foundations of this world, upon which all blessings are predicated—And when we obtain any blessing from God, it is by obedience to that law upon which it is predicated" (D&C 130:20-21). In addition, many materials from the Church use the phrase "eternal law," which implies support for an idea view of truth, where truth is expressed in abstract, universal, unchangeable ideas.

Many of God's laws may be "irrevocable" by divine decree and may have existed from before our mortal sojourn on Earth ("before the foundations of this world"), but this does not mean that they are the same sort of immutable, metaphysical entities that the Greeks referred to as absolute truth. In addition, *irrevocable* may simply mean that God's appointed laws cannot be revoked by *man's* will or authority, or that God is committed to them and will not change them at a whim. God's laws may be unchang*ing*, but that does not mean they are unchange*able*.

The Lord teaches us in the Doctrine and Covenants, for example, that *eternal* does not mean the same thing as "without end" but rather represents one of the honorific names of God:

> Nevertheless, it is not written that there shall be no end to this torment, but it is written *endless torment.*
>
> Again, it is written *eternal damnation*; wherefore it is more express than other scriptures, that it might work upon the hearts of the children of men, altogether for my name's glory.
>
> Wherefore, I will explain unto you this mystery, for it is

meet unto you to know even as mine apostles. ...

For, behold, the mystery of godliness, how great is it! For, behold, I am endless, and the punishment which is given from my hand is endless punishment, for Endless is my name. Wherefore—

Eternal punishment is *God's* punishment.

Endless punishment is *God's* punishment (D&C 19:6-8, 12, emphasis added).

Perhaps we can say something similar about "eternal law." Eternal law is *God's* law, and that is why we damage our relationship with Him when we violate it. For example, LaMar E. Garrard suggests, "[Eternal law] is eternal only in the sense that 'Eternal Law' is God's law for he created it and 'Eternal' is his name: it has a beginning and it may have an end, depending upon the circumstances."[136] It is binding upon us by virtue of the fact that it is *He* who has commanded it.

Don't modern prophets talk about moral law using Greek ideas?

Yes, modern prophets and apostles sometimes use the terms and forms of Greek thought to communicate their ideas. For example, Elder L. Tom Perry declared quite boldly: "God reveals to His prophets that there are moral absolutes. ... Surely there could not be any doctrine more strongly expressed in the scriptures than the Lord's unchanging commandments."[137] This seems to present an idea view of truth, where truth can be expressed through statements of unchangeable, abstract law.

However, in this context, Elder Perry uses Greek language to express distinctly un-Greek ideas. He speaks of God as the author and source of the commandments. He expounds, "Sin will always be sin. Disobedience to the Lord's commandments will always deprive us of His blessings."[138] In other words, focus of our moral accountability is God, a divine person. This is an idea that is foreign to Greek thought.

Further, God's commandments often do *not* change. Some instructions have remained the same from the beginning of time and will likely persist throughout all eternity. We must not harbor illusions that we can disregard God's present commandments just because they are not the immutable entities of Greek truth. Ironically, to do so would not be adhering to Hebrew thought, but rather to *Greek* thought. It is *Greek* thought that teaches us to reverence only that which is immutable. We should treat God's laws with the reverence warranted by the fact that they have been given by our Creator.

It is entirely unsurprising that prophets and apostles sometimes use the language of Greek thought in their sermons. After all, they speak English, a language of Indo-European descent, and are speaking to audiences who were also raised in the Western world and who respond positively to the language and norms of Greek thought. The language of Greek thought can communicate the weightiness and persistence of God's law—and teach us what to expect of the future on many important issues. The language of absolutism can be a powerful tool against the insidious doctrines of moral relativism.

Does the person-view of truth lead to moral relativism?

No, it does not. It is *Greek* thought that treats moral relativism as the only alternative to moral absolutism. From a person view of truth, right and wrong are centered on God and His will for us. Hebrew thought grounded morality in our covenants with God (and His covenants with us). As Richards and O'Brien helpfully note:

> Of course, relationships come with certain expectations. But if worldviews are like icebergs—with the dangerous part underwater—then in the first-century world that Paul and Jesus inhabited, relationships were the underwater part. Rules were the parts above the waterline. Rules didn't (and, in many places, still don't) describe the bulk of the matter; they merely described the visible outworking of an underlying relationship, which was the truly defining element.[139]

In other words, rules and moral principles still matter from a person view of truth. But they are surface level expressions of our deeper relationship with God.

Some will be concerned that this means that any action, no matter how violent or cruel, can become right if we think that God has commanded it. In fact, this is how violent extremists often justify murder. We have no desire to excuse them in the slightest. We do not have easy answers to these questions, except to point to Paul's statement: "But the fruit of the Spirit is love, joy, peace, longsuffering, gentleness, goodness, faith, Meekness, [and] temperance" (Galatians 5:22-23).

Any time our hearts are hardened with resentment or hate, we can guarantee that we are not acting on God's behalf. Pride, anger, and malice towards God's children alienate us from God. God is *not* going to instruct us to kill except in the direst circumstances. The more familiar we are with God's ways, the more we realize this. We read, "neither doth [the Lord] will that man should shed blood, but in all things hath forbidden it, from the beginning of man" (Ether 8:19).

God's instructions may not be the immutable abstractions of Greek thought, but detectable patterns do exist in God's teachings (and at times *strongly* so). Our point is simply that from a *person* view of truth, abstract universals are not *sufficient*. In addition, we are not left without any metric for evaluating right and wrong—we have divine revelation, we have prayer, we have reason enlightened by the Holy Spirit. We also have tradition, when that tradition is informed by a culture that acknowledges God and His servants.

References

Introduction

1. Dieter F. Uchtdorf, "Come, Join with Us," *Ensign*, November 2013, 23.

2. Ibid., 22.

3. Dallin H. Oaks, "As He Thinketh in His Heart" (address given to Church Educational System religious educators, Salt Lake City, Utah, February 8, 2013).

4. Ibid.

Chapter 1

5. *Come, Follow Me—For Individuals and Families* (Salt Lake City, UT: The Church of Jesus Christ of Latter-day Saints, 2019), 10.

6. Ezra Taft Benson, "Your Charge: To Increase In Wisdom and Favor with God and Man," *New Era*, September 1979, emphasis added.

7. James Faulconer, "Truth, Virtue, and Perspectivism," in

Virtue and the Abundant Life (Salt Lake City, UT: Deseret Book, 2012), 80.

8. Richard N. Williams, "Faithful Knowing and Virtuous Acts," in *Virtue and the Abundant Life* (Salt Lake City, Utah: Deseret Book, 2012), 62, emphasis added.

9. Brent D. Slife, "C.S. Lewis: Drawn by the Truth Made Flesh," in *C.S. Lewis, the Man and His Message: An LDS Perspective*, ed. Andrew C. Skinner and Robert L. Millett (Salt Lake City: Bookcraft, 1990), 20-37; and Brent Slife and Jeff Reber, "Comparing the Practical Implications of Secular and Christian Truth in Psychotherapy," in *Turning Freud Upside Down*, ed. Aaron P. Jackson, Lane Fischer, and Doris R. Dant (Provo: BYU Press, 2005), 160-182.

10. C. S. Lewis, *Essential C. S. Lewis* (New York, NY: Touchstone, 1996), 40.

11. Terryl L. Givens, "The Book of Mormon and Dialogic Revelation," *Journal of the Book of Mormon and Other Restoration Scripture* 10, no. 2 (2001): 20.

12. Joseph Smith, *History of the Church*, 5:134-135.

13. C.S. Lewis, *Perelandra* (New York, NY: Scribner, 1996), 64. The entire exchange between these characters is fascinating and may highlight some of the central contrasts between a Greek and Hebrew way of thinking.

14. Slife, "C.S. Lewis," 20-37.

15. Yoram Hazony, *The Philosophy of Hebrew Scripture* (Cambridge, UK: Cambridge University Press, 2012), 201.

16. C.S. Lewis, *Surprised by Joy* (Orlando, FL: Harcourt, 1955), 228-229.

17. Bruce R. McConkie, "Our Relationship with the Lord" (devotional address given at Brigham Young University, March 2, 1982).

18. First Presidency, "The Origin of Man," *Improvement Era*, November, 1909, 75–81; reprinted in *Ensign*, February, 2002.

19. C.S. Lewis, *Mere Christianity* (1952; Harper Collins: 2001), 164.

20. C. S. Lewis, *A Grief Observed* (New York, NY: HarperCollins, 1961), 78.

Chapter 2

21. Alfred North Whitehead, *Process and Reality* (New York, NY: Simon and Schuster, 2010), 39. It might also be accurate to characterize the intellectual history of the Western world as a centuries-long critical dialogue between Plato and Aristotle. For an excellent articulation of that viewpoint, see Arthur Herman's excellent book *The Cave and the Light: Plato versus Aristotle, and the Struggle for the Soul of Western Civilization* (New York, NY: Random House, 2013).

22. Norman H. Snaith, *The Distinctive Ideas of the Old Testament* (New York, NY: Schocken Books, 1964), 159.

23. John Dillenberger, "Revelational Discernment and the Problem of the Two Testaments," in Bernhard W. Anderson, ed., *The Old Testament and Christian Faith* (New York, NY: Herder and Herder, 1969), 160.

24. The distinguished philosopher Daniel Robinson explains, "The gods of Homer have their favorites among mortals and even occasionally breed with them, but in general the

Olympians are preoccupied with their own affairs, often indifferent and even contemptuous of human lives and limitations." From Daniel Robinson, *An Intellectual History of Psychology* (Madison, WI: University of Wisconsin Press, 1995), 16.

25. Daniel Robinson explains further: "[The gods of the Greeks] must be propitiated, never aroused to anger or envy. But they are also not looked to for answers to the abiding questions or for solutions to the problems of life and mind. In the matter of fundamental truths and their implications, we are left to our own devices, for, in these matters, the gods themselves are limited. Even the mighty Zeus must consult the fates if he would know the end result of his designs." From Robinson, *An Intellectual History*, 17.

26. Even Plato's Demiurge—a sort of artisan God who fashioned the world out of a chaos of pre-existing materials—was thought to be of a lesser order of perfection than the Eternal Forms, a knowledge of which the Demiurge employed in the creation of the world. See Francis M. Cornford, *Plato's Cosmology* (Indianapolis, IN: Hackett Publishing Company, 1997).

27. James Faulconer, *Scripture Study: Tools and Suggestions* (Provo, UT: BYU Press, FARMS, 1999), 136.

28. Jeffrey C. Leon, *Science and Philosophy in the West* (Upper Saddle River, NJ: Prentice-Hall, 1999).

29. For an engaging look at Aristotle's influence down through the ages, and most especially in our modern era, see Arthur Herman, *The Cave and the Light: Plato versus Aristotle, and the Struggle for the Soul of Western Civilization* (New York, NY: Random House, 2013).

30. Some might suggest that Heraclitus (535 B.C.–475 B.C.) is an exception. He is famous for having claimed that "everything flows" and "a man cannot step into the same stream twice." Heraclitus emphasized the universality of *change*. However, this exception simply highlights the rule. According to Thorlief Boman, for example, "This high estimate of change and motion is un-Greek; Heraclitus stands alone among Greek philosophers with his doctrine." In addition, Heraclitus postulated an unchanging logos that governed change in the world, and so some do not consider him an exception at all. See Thorleif Boman, *Hebrew Thought Compared with Greek*, trans. Jules L. Moreau (New York, NY: Norton, 1960), 51-52.

Further, Heraclitus's expression of his ideas was labored and difficult, largely because "the Greek language which, unlike Hebrew, was not capable of giving adequate expression to such ideas." Plato himself said of Heraclitus and his ideas, "The maintainers of this doctrine have as yet no words in which to express themselves, and must get a new language." See Boman, *Hebrew Thought*, 51-52.

31. Noel Reynolds explains this idea well: "One of the most fundamental and perennially attractive contributions of early Greek thinkers was the concept of nature—the idea that behind all the variety and vagaries of human experience there might be a solid, regular, and permanent reality. Nor did they limit this insight to the physical and material world, but rather they also glimpsed (or diligently sought) the possibility of finding ultimate truth in matters pertaining to human morality and the good." From Noel Reynolds, "The Decline of Covenant in Early Christian Thought," in Noel B. Reynolds, ed., *Early Christians in Disarray: Contemporary*

LDS Perspectives on the Christian Apostasy (Provo, UT: BYU Press, FARMS, 2005), 309.

32. James Faulconer wrote, "Though Indo-European (hereafter referred to as Greek) languages focus on the static when concerned with what ultimately is, Semitic (hereafter referred to as Hebrew) languages focus on the temporal (but they mean something different by time) and dynamic." From Faulconer, *Scripture Study*, 136.

33. Marvin Wilson, *Our Father Abraham: The Jewish Roots of the Christian Faith* (Grand Rapids, MI: William B. Eerdmans Publishing Company, 1989), 137.

34. Wilson, *Our Father Abraham*, 137.

35. George Adam Smith, "The Hebrew Genius as Exhibited in the Old Testament," in *The Legacy of Israel*, ed. Edwyn R. Bevan and Charles Singer (Oxford, UK: Clarendon Press, 1944), 10.

36. Faulconer, *Scripture Study*, 137.

37. Ibid.

38. Expanding on this point, the philosopher William Barrett has taught: "Hebraism contains no eternal realm of essences, which Greek philosophy was to fabricate. ... Such a realm of eternal essences is possible only for a detached intellect, one who, in Plato's phrase, becomes a 'spectator of all time and all existence.' This ideal of the philosopher as the highest human type—the theoretical intellect who from the vantage point of eternity can survey all time and existence—is altogether foreign to the Hebraic concept of the man of faith who is passionately committed to his own mortal being. Detachment was for the Hebrew an impermissible state of

mind, a vice rather than a virtue." From William Barrett, *Irrational Man: A Study in Existential Philosophy* (New York, NY: Anchor Books, 1990), 76.

39. Wilson, *Our Father Abraham*, 137.

40. Marvin R. Wilson, *Exploring our Hebraic Heritage: A Christian Theology of Roots and Renewal* (Grand Rapids, MI: William B. Eerdmans Publishing, 2014), 24.

41. Gerhard von Rad, *Old Testament Theology*, vol. 1, trans. D. M. G. Stalker (New York, NY: Harper and Row, 1962), 190.

42. This emphasis on the particular distinguishes Hebrew ways of thinking from Greek philosophical approaches. Thomas Cahill explains this crucial difference: "Everything about the core values of the Jews and Christians was foreign to the Greeks and Romans, who in their philosophy had decided that whatever is unique is monstrous and unintelligible ... only that which *is* forever is truly intelligible and worthy of contemplation. The ideal is what is interesting; the individual is beside the point. In contrast, for the Hebrews, the *particular* and the *contextual* was of vital interest instead." From Thomas Cahill, *Sailing the Wine-Dark Sea: Why the Greeks Matter* (New York, NY: Doubleday, 2003), 259.

43. Dallin H. Oaks, "Apostasy and Restoration," *Ensign*, May 1995, 84.

44. Boman, *Hebrew Thought*, 17.

45. For example, Noel Reynolds explains: "[A]lready in apostasy, the third-century Christians were in deep trouble. Official persecutions were increasing. They were plagued by a rapidly multiplying diversity of Christian doctrines and sects—each claiming to be the true heir of Christ and the apostles. There

was no central leadership to help them distinguish between the true and the false. ... Threatened with the utter demise of Christianity, they turned to well established and widely admired principles of Greek philosophy for a solution." From Noel Reynolds, "What Went Wrong for the Early Christians?" in Noel B. Reynolds, ed., *Early Christians in Disarray: Contemporary LDS Perspectives on the Christian Apostasy* (Provo, UT: BYU Press, FARMS, 2005), 12.

46. Religious scholar Henry Jansen explains that, over time, Christian thinkers and theologians increasingly "borrow[ed] a number of fundamental concepts from Greek philosophy, viewing the philosophies of Plato and Aristotle as most nearly approximating the Bible and using it extensively for the conceptualization of the biblical depiction of God." From Henry Jansen, *Relationality and the Concept of God* (Amsterdam, The Netherlands: Rodopi, 1995), 82.

47. Oaks, "Apostasy," 85.

48. Martin Luther, *Bondage of the Will*, trans. Henry Cole (New York, NY: Feather Trail Press, 2009), 33.

49. James Faulconer, "Appendix 2: Hebrew versus Greek Thinking," in *Scripture Study: Tools and Suggestions* (Provo, UT: BYU Press, FARMS, 1999), 136, italics added.

50. Ibid., 137.

51. Indeed, the evidence seems so compelling that it has led at least one Latter-day Saint thinker to claim, "Twenty-first Century Mormons and Hebrew Christians at the meridian of time are one and the same." From David Thomas, *Hebrew Roots of Mormonism* (Springville, UT: Cedar Fort, 2013), 247.

Additional sources include the following:

Richard E. Nisbett, *The Geography of Thought: How Asians and Westerners Think Differently ... and Why* (New York, NY: Free Press, 2003).

Murray H. Lichtenstein, "An Interpersonal Theology of the Hebrew Bible," in Alice Ogden Bellis and Joel S. Kaminsky, eds., *Jews, Christians, and the Theology of the Hebrew Scriptures* (Atlanta, GA: Society of Biblical Literature), 61-82.

Chapter 3

52. Barrett, *Irrational Man*, 76.

53. Robert Millet, "What Is Our Doctrine?" in *By Study and by Faith: Selections from the Religious Educator*, ed. Richard Holzapfel and Kent P. Jackson (Provo, UT: Religious Studies Center, Brigham Young University, 1990), 69-89.

54. James E. Faulconer, "Rethinking Theology: The Shadow of the Apocalypse," *FARMS Review* 19, no. 1 (2007), 179.

55. Bruce R. McConkie, "All Are Alike Unto God" (address given to Church Educational System religious educators, August 18, 1978).

56. Wilson, *Our Father Abraham*, 153.

57. J. Max Wilson, "Rejecting the Living Prophets by Following Future Prophets," *Sixteen Small Stones*, March 5, 2013.

Additional sources include the following:

James E. Faulconer, "Why a Mormon Won't Drink Coffee but Might Have a Coke: The Atheological Character of The Church of Jesus Christ of Latter-day Saints," *Element* 2, no. 2 (2006).

George W. Stroup, *The Promise of Narrative Theology: Recovering the Gospel in the Church* (Eugene, OR: Wipf and Stock Publishers, 1997).

Stanley Hauerwas & L. Gregory Jones, eds., *Why Narrative?: Readings in Narrative Theology* (Eugene, OR: Wipf and Stock Publishers, 1997).

Chapter 4

58. *Young Women Manual 3* (Salt Lake City, UT: The Church of Jesus Christ of Latter-day Saints, 1994), 6-8.

59. Sam Harris, *The End of Faith: Religion, Terror, and the Future of Reason* (New York, NY: W. W. Norton and Company, 2005), 65.

60. Brit, September 10, 2013 (3:50 pm), comment on J. Max Wilson, "Vectors—Faith and Doubt Are Incompatible in the LDS Church," *Sixteen Small Stones*, September 3, 2013, http://www.sixteensmallstones.org/vectors-faith-and-doubt-are-incompatible-in-the-lds-church/

61. Cody Hatch, "The Necessity of Doubt," *Wheat & Tares*, January 16, 2019, https://wheatandtares.org/2019/01/16/the-necessity-of-doubt/

62. C.S. Lewis, *The World's Last Night: And Other Essays* (Orlando, FL: Harcourt, 1960), 26.

63. James Faulconer, "Truth, Virtue, and Perspectivism," in *Virtue and the Abundant Life* (Salt Lake City, UT: Deseret Book, 2012), 85.

64. Marvin Wilson, *Our Father Abraham: The Jewish Roots of the Christian Faith* (Grand Rapids, MI: William B. Eerdmans Publishing Company, 1989), 184.

Chapter 5

65. *Teachings of Presidents of the Church: Joseph Smith,* (Salt Lake City, UT: The Church of Jesus Christ of Latter-day Saints, 2011), 206-216.

66. Lewis, *Perelandra,* 208.

67. C.S. Lewis, *The Silver Chair* (New York, NY: HarperCollins, 1953), 20-21.

68. C.S. Lewis, *The Lion, the Witch, and the Wardrobe* (New York, NY: HarperCollins, 1950), 86.

69. Lewis, *A Grief Observed,* 20.

70. Ibid., 78.

71. Reynolds, "The Decline," 319, emphasis added.

72. Attributed to Robert Keen, "How Firm a Foundation," in *Hymns of The Church of Jesus Christ of Latter-day Saints* (Salt Lake City, UT: The Church of Jesus Christ of Latter-day Saints, 1985), hymn #85.

Chapter 6

73. See, for example, Edward J. Brandt, "The Tabernacle of Ancient Israel," *Ensign,* November, 1973, 36-38, or Sidney B. Sperry, "Ancient Temples and Their Functions," *Ensign,* January, 1972, 67-72.

74. Alan Hirshfeld, *Eureka Man: The Life and Legacy of Archimedes* (New York, NY: Walker & Company, 2009).

Additional sources include the following:

Richard Williams, "Faith, Reason, Knowledge, Truth" (devotional address given at Brigham Young University, February 1, 2000).

Parker Palmer, *To Know as We Are Known* (New York, NY: HarperCollins, 1983).

Chapter 7

75. Lewis, *Essential*, p. 39.

76. The Lord told the brother of Jared, "I will go before thee into a land which is choice above all the lands of the earth" (Ether 1:42).

77. The Lord told Nephi, "And inasmuch as ye shall keep my commandments, ye shall prosper, and shall be led to a land of promise; yea, even a land which I have prepared for you; yea, a land which is choice above all other lands" (1 Nephi 2:20).

78. Ronald K. Esplin, "A 'Place Prepared' in the Rockies," *Ensign*, July, 1988, 6-13.

79. See Hugh Nibley, *Approaching Zion* (Salt Lake City, UT: Deseret Book, 1989).

80. See Ralph Hancock's critique of this view in his article, "Our One-sided 'Openness' to Continuing Revelation," *First Things*, October 16, 2013.

81. John Dehlin, personal Facebook post (publicly visible to all users of Facebook). At the time of this writing, John Dehlin claimed to be a member of the Church in good standing.

82. A famous account of an exchange between President Abraham Lincoln and a minister during the height of the Civil War reflects this sentiment. Apparently the minister expressed to President Lincoln his fervent belief that "the Lord was on our side." The President responded: "I am not at all concerned about that, for I know that the Lord is *always* on the side of the *right*. But it is my constant anxiety and prayer that

I and this *nation* should be on the Lord's *side.*" From Francis Bicknell Carpenter, *Six Months at the White House with Abraham Lincoln* (Bedford, MA: Applewood Books, 1866), 282, italics in the original.

Chapter 8

83. For more detailed analyses of scientific and rational authority, see, e.g., Jean E. Hampton, *The Authority of Reason* (Cambridge, UK: Cambridge University Press, 1998); Theodore L. Brown, *Imperfect Oracle: The Epistemic and Moral Authority of Science* (University Park, PA: The Pennsylvania State University Press, 2009); Heather E. Douglas, *Science, Policy, and the Value-Free Ideal* (Pittsburgh, PA: The University of Pittsburgh Press, 2009).

84. See, for example, the claim in Brigham Young University's physical science textbook: "In cases of conflicting claims of knowledge between competing authorities, we often give precedence to those ... that are held to be true by the greatest number and so have been validated by the most witnesses." From J. Ward Moody, "Knowledge, Science, and the Universe," in *Physical Science Foundations* (Provo: BYU Academic Publishing, 2006), 8.

85. For a detailed analysis of the history of rational theology and creedalism in Christianity, see Jaroslav Pelikan, *Credo: Historical and Theological Guide to Creeds and Confessions of Faith in the Christian Tradition* (New Haven, CT: Yale University Press, 2003); Roger E. Olson, *The Story of Christian Theology: Twenty Centuries of Tradition and Reform* (Downers Grove, IL: InterVarsity Press, 1999); Vittorio Hosle, *God as Reason: Essays in Philosophical Theology* (Notre Dame, IN:

University of Notre Dame Press, 2013).

86. See, e.g., Hosle, *God as Reason*.

87. Faulconer, "Rethinking Theology," 180.

88. Jeffrey R Holland, "Prophets in the Land Again," *Ensign*, November, 2006, 106.

89. See also Boyd K. Packer, "The Weak and Simple of the Church," *Ensign*, November, 2007, 6-9.

90. Truman G. Madsen, *Joseph Smith the Prophet* (Salt Lake City, UT: Bookcraft, 1989), 7.

91. Brigham Young, *Journal of Discourses*, 9:150.

92. Joseph Smith, *History of the Church*, 5:265.

93. Uchtdorf, "Come, Join," 2013, 22.

Chapter 9

94. James E. Faust, "The Great Imitator," *Ensign*, November, 1987.

95. Ibid.

Chapter 10

96. E. Randolph Richards and Brandon J. O'Brien, *Misreading Scripture with Western Eyes: Removing Cultural Blinders to Better Understand the Bible* (Downers Grove, IL: InterVarsity Press, 2012), 161.

97. Julian Marias, *History of Philosophy*, trans. Stanley Appelbaum and Clarence C. Stowbidge (New York, NY: Dover, 1967), 295.

98. See, e.g., John Finnis, *Moral Absolutes: Tradition, Revision,*

and Truth (Washington, DC: The Catholic University of America, 1991); Sam Harris, *The Moral Landscape: How Science Can Determine Human Values* (New York, NY: Simon & Schuster, 2010); Samuel J. Kerstein, *Kant's Search for the Supreme Principle of Morality* (Cambridge, UK: Cambridge University Press, 2004).

99. Richards and O'Brien, *Misreading Scripture*, 161.

100. Ezra Taft Benson, "Beware of Pride," *Ensign*, May, 1989, 4.

101. Ibid.

Chapter 11

102. Lewis, *Mere Christianity*, 54-56.

103. See Thomas R. Schreiner, "Penal Substitution View," in *The Nature of the Atonement: Four Views*, ed. James Beilby and Paul R. Eddy (Downers Grove, IL: InterVarsity Press, 2006), 67-116.

104. Lewis, *Mere Christianity*, 56.

105. Theodore M. Burton, "The Meaning of Repentance," *Ensign*, August, 1988, 6-9.

Additional sources include the following:

Sir Arthur Henry King, "Atonement: The Only Wholeness," *Ensign*, April, 1975, 12-18.

Chapter 12

106. Edwin Arthur Burtt, *The Metaphysical Foundations of Modern Physical Science* (Amherst, NY: Humanity Books, 1999), 75.

107. Ibid., 173.

108. Ibid. While some Latter-day Saints have embraced Boyle's assertion here, we think there are good reasons to be cautious about this approach.

109. Moody, "Knowledge, Science," 8.

110. Brigham Young, *Journal of Discourses*, vol. 9, 168.

111. John Taylor, *Journal of Discourses*, vol. 13, 224. President Taylor went on to say, "It also reveals another grand principle, that the laws of nature are immutable and unchangeable as are all the works of God." We would argue that his use of the terms "immutable and unchangeable" should be qualified in the same way as his quotes from the previous chapter—that is, the fact that they are works of God means that they are *not* "immutable" in the same sort of way that Greek truth is. It simply means that *we* cannot change them, just as we cannot change (by our own volition) *any* of the laws of God.

112. Latter-day Saint thinker Duane Boyce notes, "We probably cannot know the extent to which we find certain intellectual viewpoints repugnant primarily because of professional stigma rather than because of our acquaintance with actual disconfirming data. Nor can we probably know the opposite—the degree to which other intellectual viewpoints hold us in their thrall simply because they are accepted by people we admire and not, again, because of our acquaintance with any actual evidence. ...

"Moreover, is impossible to know the degree to which we are cognitively captive to any number of worldviews and to trace all of the limitations and errors, large or small, that are entailed by this unavoidable, but constricting, reality of intellectual life. ... By ignoring them we are apt, in our naïveté, to ascribe more certainty than is warranted at any given moment to a particular discipline's range of intellectual conclusions ... and to risk developing an attitude of dogmatism and defensiveness as a result." From Duane Boyce, "Of Science, Scripture, and Surprise," *FARMS Review* 20, no. 2 (2008), 199.

113. Boyce, "Of Science," 199.

114. Indeed, addressing this very feature of human reason, the famous 18th Century political thinker Edmund Burke once trenchantly noted, "on the whole one may observe, that there is rather less difference upon matters of taste among mankind, than upon most of those which depend upon the naked reason; and that men are far better agreed on the excellence of a description in Virgil, than on the truth or falsehood of a theory in Aristotle." From Edmund Burke, *Philosophical Inquiry into the Origins of our Ideas of the Sublime and the Beautiful* (Oxford, UK: Oxford University Press, 2008), 23.

115. Williams, "Faith, Reason."

Conclusion

116. Matthew Arnold, *Culture and Anarchy* (New York, NY: Cambridge University Press, 1993), 126.

117. Slife and Reber, "Comparing," 167.

118. Faulconer, "Why a Mormon," 29.

Appendix A

119. Jess Feist, Gregory J. Feist, and Tomi-Ann Roberts, *Theories of Personality*, 8th Edition (Dubuque, IA: McGraw-Hill, 2012), 4.

120. Faulconer, *Scripture Study*, 140-141.

121. Dallin H. Oaks, "The Challenge to Become," *Ensign*,

November, 2000.

122. Jeff A. Benner, *The Ancient Hebrew Lexicon of the Bible* (College Station, TX: VBW Publishing, 2005), 50, 56. It should be noted that some of Benner's etymological constructions are in dispute as he is not a credentialed scholar of Semitic languages. His work represents the outcome of intense individual study of the Hebrew language and ancient culture as a personal hobby.

123. Thomas S. Monson, "See Others as They May Become," *Ensign*, November 2012, 69-70.

Appendix B

124. John A. Widstoe, *Joseph Smith as Scientist* (Heber City, UT: Archive Publishers, 2000), 138.

125. Parley P. Pratt, *Spirituality: Key to the Science of Theology* (Springville, UT: Cedar Fort, 2007), 25. He further wrote, "Among the popular errors of modern times an opinion prevails that miracles are events which transpire contrary to the laws of nature, that they are effects without a cause. If such is the fact, then, there never has been a miracle, and there never will be one. The laws of nature are the laws of *truth*. Truth is unchangeable, independent in its own sphere. A law of nature never has been broken. And it is an absolute impossibility that such a law ever should be broken. That which at first sight appears to be contrary to the known laws of nature, will always be found, on investigation, to be in perfect accordance with those laws." From Pratt, *Spirituality*, 67).

126. B. H. Roberts, *New Witnesses for God*, vol. 1, (Salt Lake City, UT: Deseret News, 1911), 249.

127. LaMar E. Garrard, "Creation, Fall, and Atonement," in *Studies in Scripture: Volume Seven: 1 Nephi to Alma 29*, ed. Kent P. Jackson (Salt Lake City, UT: Deseret Book, 1987), 93.

128. *Teachings of the Presidents of the Church: Brigham Young* (Salt Lake City, UT: The Church of Jesus Christ of Latterday Saints, 1997), 197.

129. Brigham Young, *Journal of Discourses*, 13:306.

130. Brigham Young, *Journal of Discourses*, 15:127.

131. Joseph Smith, *History of the Church*, 4:554.

132. Joseph Smith, *Teachings of the Prophet Joseph Smith*, 345, emphasis added.

133. Faulconer, "Appendix 2," 141.

134. D. Todd Christofferson, "Free Forever, to Act for Themselves," *Ensign*, November, 2014, 18.

135. Jaroslav Pelikan, *The Christian Tradition: A History of the Development of Doctrine* (Chicago, IL: University of Chicago, 1971), 22.

136. LaMar E. Garrard, "God, Natural Law, and the Doctrine and Covenants," in *Doctrines for Exaltation: Sidney B. Sperry Symposium*, February, 1989 (Salt Lake City, UT: Deseret Book, 1989), 69.

137. L. Tom Perry, "Obedience to Law Is Liberty," *Ensign*, May, 2013, 88.

138. Ibid.

139. Richards and O'Brien, *Misreading Scripture*, 161.

Made in the USA
Las Vegas, NV
11 January 2024